F

THE CROWDFUNDING BOOK

If you have a business dream and need a little (or a lot) of cash to get it going, Patty Lennon's insights will be invaluable.

SHAWN HULL
Successful Crowdfunder and Owner, Hull's Happiest Days Designs

Until I read Patty Lennon's book, I always thought of crowdfunding as a way to raise money. Once I understood her approach I saw the tremendous marketing potential of crowdfunding. I can't think of a better or more cost-effective way to build a community of people who support you and your message.

ANGELA LAURIA
President, The Author Incubator

Patty Lennon is brilliant at blending intuition with specific action plans to create massive success. This book will help anyone even thinking of launching a crowdfunding campaign!

ANGELA JIA KIM
founder of the Savor Lifestyle brands

Patty Lennon takes the mystery out of crowdfunding in *The Crowdfunding Book*. Her practical and engaging approach will help thousands of people launch successful campaigns and raise the funds to realize their dreams.

BRENDA BAZAN AND NANCY HAYES
CoFounders, MoolaHoop

THE CROWDFUNDING BOOK

A how-to book for
entrepreneurs, writers & inventors.

Patty Lennon

DISCLAIMER

Neither the author nor the publisher assumes any responsibility for errors, omissions, or contrary interpretations of the subject matter herein. Any perceived slight of any individual or organization is purely unintentional.

Brand and product names are trademarks or registered trademarks of their respective owners.

Editing: Kris Kane & Richard Heby

Cover Design: Ann Alger

Interior Book Design: Heidi Miller

To Matthew and Katie,
my first, last and always.

TABLE OF
CONTENTS

1

Introduction

9

Chapter One
SETTING UP FOR SUCCESS

35

Chapter Two
MARKETING STRATEGIES

57

Chapter Three
CREATING YOUR PITCH VIDEO

89

Chapter Four
STRUCTURING YOUR FUNDING

99

Chapter Five
THE POWER OF YOUR INNER CIRCLE

121

Chapter Six
YOUR ONLINE CAMPAIGN

137

Chapter Seven
YOUR MARKETING PLAN

165

Chapter Eight
THE EASY MONEY MINDSET

177

Chapter Nine
GET READY, GET SET...LAUNCH!

189

Resources

193

Contributors

197

Acknowledgements

199

About the Author

INTRODUCTION

Some say, it takes money to make money. So what do you do when you have a great idea but no money to invest in it?

In January of 2012 I was looking out at the landscape of a new year wondering how in the world I was going to make my goals a reality (or bring my business dreams to life). The previous couple of years had thrown our family a few curve balls that affected our financial stability.

My husband lost his job the year prior and I was the primary caretaker for my mom, who was diagnosed with lung cancer. At the time my children were three and five years old. I wanted to be with them at least some of their waking hours, so working around the clock was out of the option.

My focus was to grow revenue while managing the money we spent to create that revenue.

One of my biggest goals was to launch the Mom Gets A Business Conference to support women who wanted to grow businesses while raising their families. This issue hit close to home as I watched more and more people go through what our family struggled with—a spouse out of work.

Every part of me knew that I had to bring this event to life. Unfortunately the price to bring that conference into the world was $45,000, and I wasn't willing to take that kind of risk with our family's finances.

Although my business was growing considerably, I was still in the early stages of business development. I was investing much of my profit back into the business to help it grow. At the same time I was supporting a double income household on the single income of my business.

Pulling $45,000 from our family's savings just didn't feel like the right decision for us then.

I was sharing this struggle with my mastermind group when one of the women suggested crowdfunding. At the time I only had a vague understanding of what crowdfunding actually was. Little did I know that one conversation would dramatically and amazingly transform my business and my life in ways I couldn't have possibly imagined.

When I made the decision to use crowdfunding to raise the funds for the Mom Gets A Business Conference, I considered every conceivable fear about crowdfunding.

> *What if no one funds me?*
>
> *What if people judge me?*
>
> *How in God's name do I ask my friends and family for money and show my face at the next Thanksgiving dinner?*
>
> *What if people think I'm poor?*

I'm embarrassed about this last one but I share it openly here because I have spoken with many potential crowdfunders and I find that this fear holds back too many people from accessing the tremendous power of crowdfunding.

If you fear, that by crowdfunding, people will think you are poor or are struggling—then I have a wake up call for you: the majority of human beings in the world live in abject poverty. It is just sad that we fear we might be perceived as someone who needs money. If you have the resources to access this book you have more than most human beings on the planet do right now. Please don't waste another minute worrying about what other people think.

I say this with love and compassion because it is exactly the reality check I wish I could have given myself early on in the process.

I'm guessing the reason you even picked up this book is because you have an incredible gift to share with the world—a solution that will help improve people's lives—and that gift, needs cash to grow. Are you really going to let the fear of what others might think keep you from sharing your gift with the world?

No. Of course you won't.

And even if that niggling little fear of what others might think still hangs out in the back of your mind, I can tell you that, standing on the other side of my own successful campaign, those fears do nothing to help you.

I've worked with and interviewed many crowdfunders and I can tell you that those of us that followed the process outlined in this book walked away from the crowdfunding experience with many gifts. One of the greatest gifts is knowing how many people believed in us and were willing to support us.

Learning how many people have your back is reason enough to launch a campaign (in my personal opinion). But beyond that, there is a reason well established companies (not poor people) use crowdfunding every day to launch products and grow their customer base. They've discovered the **secret power of crowdfunding** that few people understand. It's the secret I discovered while successfully running my own campaign: crowdfunding is not about the money!

Well that's not 100% true. Of course successful crowdfunding raises the money you need to bring your dream to life. But the true value of crowdfunding is its marketing power.

Crowdfunding is *the most* powerful marketing machine in our world today. It creates social proof, raises capital, creates customer engagement, generates market research and integrates the value of your social connections to what you are creating in a direct and tangible way.

One of the greatest gifts—especially for entrepreneurs and creative people who are still in the early stages of development—is that crowdfunding gives your supporters, allies, friends, and family a way to market for you.

Before launching my crowdfunding campaign I had a number of people in my life that wanted to support me, but there was little they could do to help. Either they didn't know my target client, didn't understand what I did, or simply didn't know how to communicate it.

When I launched my campaign all those people suddenly had a clear and simple way to support what I was doing. The crowdfunding campaign page and pitch video I created did all the communication work for them; all my supporters needed to do was direct traffic to the campaign and our campaign page did the rest of the leg work.

The pitch video also helped my supporters connect to the vision I had for my big dream (the Mom Gets A Business Conference) in a way that just wasn't typically possible in brief social interactions.

Beyond allowing you to harness the power of your inner circle, crowdfunding shows you the demand for your product or creation because people vote with their dollars. So you learn what people are willing to pay for before you invest *your* dollars. When your campaign is live you can test new messaging, product enhancements, and price points to uncover everything you need to know to make what you are producing a success.

Take Mark Bollman, founder of Ball & Buck, a successful niche-clothing retailer. Mark and I met a few months ago, speaking on a crowdfunding panel at Harvard. He told the audience that he has used crowdfunding to launch multiple products and will continue to do so precisely because of its marketing power. In his words:

From a market and engagement standpoint there is no better choice for us. We are in a close, collaborative engagement with our end user. We now have 1200 additional customers because of our campaign, which is incredible. And while the campaign is running we are getting real-time feedback of what the customer would need to see to make our products ideal for them. We've secured PR because of our campaigns. We understand what we need to do to be great in the eyes of our ideal customer.

Ball & Buck is not the only successful company to harness the power of crowdfunding. You can find a perfect example of the marketing value of crowdfunding with the campaign that, at the time this book was written, was the largest fixed funding campaign ever! It also failed to raise even half of its funding target.

On August 21, 2013 the Ubuntu Edge ended its campaign having raised $12,814,216 in contributions and then gave it all back since it failed to reach its $32,000,000 target. Two days later their founder Mark Shuttleworth espoused the marketing value Ubuntu received from the campaign stating on their blog:

All of the support and publicity has continued to drive our discussions with some major manufacturers, and we have many of the world's biggest mobile networks already signed up to the Ubuntu Carrier Advisory Group.

Shuttleworth thanked their supporters saying:

> Many of you gave your time as well as money, organising your own mailing lists, social media strategies and online ads, and successfully reaching out to your local media. We even saw entire sites created to gather information and help promote the Edge.

You can receive that same level of support from your own communities and social connections! Maybe you won't raise $12 million dollars but if you set a realistic goal (we'll talk more about how to do that later) you can do better than the Ubuntu Edge campaign by funding 100% or more of your targeted amount.

Let's get started!

CHAPTER ONE
SETTING UP FOR SUCCESS

In this chapter you will be laying the groundwork before Day One of your campaign so the dollars flow from the moment you start your crowdfunding initiative.

Choosing a Platform

There are a wide variety of platform options out there. Two of the better-known platforms are Kickstarter and Indiegogo. Both of these sites serve a variety of demographics, categories, and project types.

There are also a number of niche sites. They offer specialized services focused on a specific demographic, project, or product type. For example, Publaunch is dedicated to writers and publishers and what they produce. PlumAlley exclusively focuses on women innovators and leaders and connecting them to capital to grow their ventures. Other platforms serve the arts, veterans, personal projects, causes, etc.

There are over 1000 crowdfunding platforms in various states of development, and that number grows daily. Niche platforms show tremendous potential for the future of crowdfunding. However, when I wrote this book only a small percentage of niche crowdfunding sites have shown significant contribution to the success of their targeted community's campaigns.

Stay open minded as you consider which platform to choose for your campaign. Follow the exercises in this chapter to guide you. Most importantly, follow your gut.

Your platform is not responsible for driving traffic to your campaign—you are. If you hope to launch your campaign and have strangers miraculously find you and fund you, then I'm here to burst that bubble. That just isn't how crowdfunding works.

Platforms do feature a small percentage of campaigns in emails and on home pages. While this can drive traffic and contributions from people outside your network, I don't recommend building your crowdfunding campaign on this expectation.

I don't know of any aspect of an individual platform that makes it objectively better than any other for crowdfunding. As each platform matures and finds new ways to drive independent traffic to campaigns that might change. Still, this hasn't happened yet; and you shouldn't rely on crowdfunding platforms to drive traffic and contribution.

Choosing a platform is more about a gut feeling than statistics. Few reliable statistics even exist. Crowdfunding is just too new. If your goal is to be featured on a campaign platform (and in turn take advantage of that platform's visitors) you will probably want to pay attention to one metric that can be reliably tracked. That is web traffic.

To compare the traffic of various sites, you can visit alexa. com and enter the name of the site you're considering. This will give you some basic traffic statistics. You'll pull up a screen like this one:

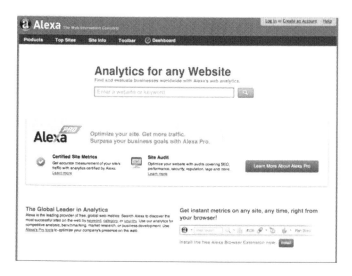

(You can find a description of how Alexa rankings work here: pattylennon.com/alexa-traffic.)

You can input any URL on the Alexa page and it will show you a page's overall rank compared to other sites. The lower the number, the more traffic that website URL gets.

Not surprisingly, the two most well known platforms Kickstarter and Indiegogo experience the most traffic. That sort of recognition can be important if you are planning to pursue media coverage as a critical part of your campaign strategy. Most mainstream media has a basic understanding of crowdfunding but when I speak with reporters they typically only know the names "Kickstarter" and "Indiegogo." If you are pitching media to share your story it may help you get featured if the journalist you reach recognizes the name of your platform.

That being said, I've also seen the founders of smaller niche sites get personally involved in helping to feature their site's campaigns in media because that helps increase the platform's visibility.

Getting to know the various crowdfunding sites on a deeper level will help you make your decision. The exercises in this chapter are designed to help you through that process.

Let's start with an overview of just a handful of the 1000+ platforms available for your consideration:

1. Kickstarter *kickstarter.com*

Kickstarter was launched in 2009 to fund creative projects under such categories as art, design, film, games, music, food, and photography, among others. However, Kickstarter is not the platform for causes, charities, businesses and personal funding. Open to those based in the US, the UK, Canada, Australia and New Zealand, Kickstarter has funded over 50,000 projects with 44% of them reaching their funding goals.

2. Indiegogo *indiegogo.com*

Indiegogo is all about funding your passion—it could be related to technology, health, design, film, the environment, or even giving someone a vacation. An international crowdfunding platform, it has raised millions of dollars for thousands of campaigns since launching in 2007. Provide your passion, and Indiegogo's supportive community provides the necessary tools for your campaign to "raise funds quickly, easily and securely."

3. PubLaunch *publaunch.com*

PubLaunch strives to give all writers a chance to publish their books by providing access to services tailored specifically to the writers' needs. It starts with a crowdfunding platform but it doesn't end there. PubLaunch combines crowdfunding with a collaborative work environment that connects writers with the trusted industry professionals they need to make their book a success.

4. MoolaHoop *moola-hoop.com*

This crowdfunding site helps women entrepreneurs start and grow their small businesses. Once funding goals have been met, supporters of the project will receive rewards such as special discounts on products or services. MoolaHoop is currently open to entrepreneurs based in the US.

5. Appbackr *appbackr.com*

Totally techie in nature, Appbackr is a digital marketplace that helps mobile app developers find backers willing to help fund their applications. A developer sells an app on the site, and the backer purchases a bulk amount of this app for potential profit. After apps get sold on the mobile app store, Appbackr then receives payment and distributes profits to all investing parties.

6. Fundable *fundable.com*

Fundable is the go-to crowdfunding platform for small businesses. Its funding is investment-based, where backers receive either rewards or equity. An "all-or-nothing" platform, Fundable gives startups enough time to build momentum around their campaign, which is usually 60 to 90 days.

7. Crowdfunder *crowdfunder.com*

Crowdfunder is now exclusively focused on investment-based transactions although it originally offered a blend of donation-based and investment based transactions. The site connects entrepreneurs of small businesses and social enterprises with investors through a growing global social network. Unique to this platform is CROWDFUNDx— an initiative in cities across the US and Mexico where local business owners have the opportunity to meet nearby angel investors in both online and offline live events.

8. RocketHub *rockethub.com*

RocketHub is an innovative crowdfunding platform that brings fun into the mix. Open to global "project leaders" in art, business, science, and social enterprises, it provides clear guidelines on how to launch a campaign in their Success School. They've also partnered with governments, educators, and communities to ensure your project's success.

8. Plum Alley *plumalley.co*

Plum Alley is a site where women raise money. Founded in 2012, Plum Alley works with women from diverse sectors to help bring their entrepreneurial ideas to life. Their easy-to-use crowdfunding platform enables women to raise money online from their networks and beyond, and has attracted an engaged community of men and women who are committed to investing in women's success.

10. Hatchfund *hatchfund.org*

Hatchfund is a thriving creative community that funds projects geared towards the arts—from the disciplines of architecture and design to theater and visual arts, from dance to literature to music. A charitable organization, Hatchfund offers a patent-pending matching fund program for its artists. Seventy-five percent of the company's projects have been successfully funded. Its rationale is that art makes valuable contributions to our lives, communities and cultures, which is why it deserves to be supported.

11. GoFundMe *gofundme.com*

GoFundMe supports personal causes and life events such as school tuition, medical bills, sports teams, volunteer trips, travel expenses, and even pets! GoFundMe has helped thousands of people; the site prides itself on creating a warm community feel. This is a great option for personal fundraising or "cause" campaigns. Choose from the following campaigns: Personal Donation, Charity Fundraising, and All-or-Nothing crowdfunding.

I am constantly researching and interviewing founders of different crowdfunding platforms to understand their motivation for launching crowdfunding sites, and to get their take on where crowdfunding is and where it is going.

Most crowdfunding platforms are still small businesses themselves, where the founders are intimately involved in the day-to-day work of their platform. Understanding who these people are and why they do what they do may be helpful in choosing the platform to launch your campaign.

Although I could never include summaries of what I've found on every platform here are some of those you may be interested in:

KICKSTARTER

Kickstarter is arguably the most widely recognized crowdfunding platform for two reasons. One, because it was one of the first crowdfunding platforms; two because it has garnered media attention from around the world. Kickstarter is one of the few platforms that allows campaigns from countries outside the U.S.—a trait that has contributed to its worldwide media success.

Kickstarter could be called the "granddaddy" of crowdfunding because of its numbers. Since its launch in April 2009, Kickstarter has funded over 55,000 projects, and over 5.7 million people have pledged funds totaling more than $1 billion.

Why It Was Created

Perry Chen first had the idea for crowdfunding when he wanted to create a show during the 2002 New Orleans Jazz Fest. He had the DJs picked out, and a venue, but not enough money to make it happen. The crowdfunding concept for music was born: let the audience decide if something should happen by having them pledge to buy tickets.

After moving back to New York, his idea prospered. In 2005, Perry met Yancey Strickler, a music journalist, who helped plan the site, and then a year later, Charles Adler joined the duo in the preliminary planning stages. Over the next few years, the team grew and Kickstarter finally launched.

What It Funds

Kickstarter has always been project-based. While it started primarily as a music project funding tool, it has expanded to fund other arts including theater, film, dance, art, comics, design, photography, technology, games, and publishing.

Kickstarter often turns down campaigns because they aren't project-based, and the platform is primarily creatively-focused: for artists, performers, and creators, rather than for start-up funding for small businesses. While the site often funds video games, considering them projects, Kickstarter usually rejects websites or apps for ecommerce, business, and social networking projects. Companies can fund a product or project, but not generate funds to start a company or service.

How To Succeed

Kickstarter definitely has a lot of traffic because it is so well known. The downside to this fact is that if a campaign is well known and fails, that makes for some bad press. While that may not affect most campaigns, there has been backlash when famous actors or filmmakers try to fund their new film project. When Zach Braff started a campaign to film a project that studios had passed on, he raised the money in 48 hours and then got pushback from the public because of it.

Being famous doesn't make one successful. Zosia Mamet, an actress on one of the most watched series on television, Girls, recently tried to fund a music video and fell short of her target. She didn't even raise 10% of her goal. Obviously fame isn't the magic ingredient.

But like any crowdfunding campaign, success is not based on luck. It is based on marketing your project and using social media to drive it. The numbers prove that as well. While over 55,000 have been funded, over 71,000 have failed.

However, even some campaigns that fail still win, perhaps not with dollars, but with exposure. The platform serves as more than a funding tool for artists and creators. It exposes them to a wide audience and the statistics prove that.

MOOLA-HOOP

Former IBM executives Brenda Bazan and Nancy Hayes co-founded Moola-Hoop, a crowdfunding site for women entrepreneurs. I reached out to Brenda and Nancy because I was intrigued by their focus of creating support for women entrepreneurs while they are growing their businesses, not just during the crowdfunding process.

How Moola-Hoop Started

Brenda and Nancy knew each other from their days at IBM. Both women had moved into spaces where they worked with women entrepreneurs and collectively they saw the struggle that women entrepreneurs faced in getting funding to start a business and grow it. They studied the statistics and found that women lead 30% of new business start-ups, yet women receive only 5% of venture capital and only 12% of institutional funding.

Brenda and Nancy pinpointed an advantage women have in business—being great networkers—so they decided to nurture that trait in order to close the gender gap.

How Moola-Hoop Works

The crowdfunding site is built for female-owned businesses, primarily those with consumer facing products. Before creating a campaign, Moola-Hoop provides tips to help women create a successful crowdfunding plan by encouraging them to present a business idea with photos, videos, and select rewards to funders, including deals on their products or services, or unique experiences at each level of contribution.

One belief that Brenda and Nancy emphasize is that crowdfunding isn't only about raising money. It's also great product/market validation and provides women with valuable feedback from customers and builds support for products before they hit the marketplace.

Rather than an all-or-nothing goal like many crowdfunding platforms, Moola-Hoop allows women to articulate milestones such as what will be accomplished with the first $10,000, and the next $15,000. Once a campaign reaches a milestone, the campaign is funded up to that amount to allow access to funding. While some platforms provide either fixed or flexible funding with variable fees, Moola-Hoop's milestone funding campaign fee is the same percentage as a fixed campaign.

What's Next?

Brenda and Nancy have plans to expand past crowdfunding by providing greater access to tips, resources, solutions, attorneys, social media experts, community connections, and mentors. Their vision is like match.com but to connect women who need to fill specific needs. For example a young woman might be looking for a mentor, while a more experienced woman may be looking for a partner or someone who provides complimentary services. A retail business owner may connect with a location for a pop-up shop.

PUBLAUNCH

How PubLaunch Started

PubLaunch started out of necessity. As an editor and publisher, Greg Ioannou (PubLaunch's president and founder) realized that existing resources only provide a part of the picture. PubLaunch came to life to provide all the services a writer needs in one place, along with all the information and tools you need to get published.

Crowdfunding became a natural part of the picture because it allows writers to market test their book before publication. If a book succeeds at crowdfunding, it will most likely sell well. If it doesn't, then the author has valuable information about the book's marketability without having gone to the expense of paying to get it published.

How PubLaunch Works

PubLaunch is a combination of crowdfunding platform and industry marketplace. The crowdfunding platform is integrated with the other services or tools, allowing a writer to connect with and hire vetted industry professionals and pay for their services using crowdfunding. The idea is to make the entire publishing process (from hiring freelancers to managing the project to marketing the book) as easy to use and seamless as possible.

What Makes PubLaunch Different

PubLaunch stands apart from existing services because it provides tools and services for every part of the book-publishing project. From working draft to finished product, the site guides authors through each phase and connects them with the necessary services all in one place. Combining the marketplace with crowdfunding was a natural step for Publaunch that also sets them apart from other services. Publaunch founders see it as an essential part of publishing for a lot of authors.

What's Next for PubLaunch

PubLaunch will continue to grow its marketplace and ecosystem. Publaunch wants to make the workflow between the book publishing world and crowdfunding as seamless as possible and will continue to work on new features to improve their functionality to make that happen.

What's Next for Crowdfunding

Crowdfunding is really becoming a means to an end. It's the first step in a process that helps people to get their life-long dreams off the ground while allowing them to maintain full control of their projects. Publaunch is seeing people start businesses and sell equity through crowdfunding. PubLaunch is among the first to integrate crowdfunding as a major part of an industry process, but expects to see others heading in that direction in the future.

PLUM ALLEY

When Plum Alley launched in 2012 its focus was not on crowdfunding but on showcasing the contributions women were making as innovators, in tech and as entrepreneurs. As the site grew those same women innovators and leaders communicated a need to raise capital to grow their ventures. In 2013 founder Deborah Jackson invested in building a platform that would demystify this process, grounded in her own capital-raising expertise.

How It Started

Deborah Jackson says she started Plum Alley "because I wanted to advance women entrepreneurs, because we need the products and companies they are creating to exist in the world. We need to engage both women and men to find meaningful ways to support businesses founded by women and gender diverse teams."

How It Works

Plum Alley features companies founded by women and gender diverse teams. While they don't have a specific industry focus, Plum Alley likes to profile companies that are having a profound and transformative impact in the world. More specifically, Plum Alley crowdfunding offers non-equity crowdfunding opportunities for female entrepreneurs to grow their businesses.

What Makes Plum Alley Different

When I asked Deborah how she differentiates Plum Alley from the growing number of crowdfunding platforms she named three key areas:

1. Personal support and guidance throughout the crowdfunding process.

2. A custom built site developed to provide specific advice at each stage of your campaign.

3. Higher success rate: Campaigns on Plum Alley have succeeded at a rate more than twice the industry average.

What is Next?

The SEC has just released regulations that allow non-accredited investors to participate in investing in startups and companies. In the next few months we could likely see a rise in the number of equality crowdfunding sites that offer opportunities to non-accredited investors.

Deborah says Plum Alley "will continue to offer our non-equity crowdfunding to companies founded by women and gender diverse teams. However, because we have met so many outstanding women entrepreneurs that need and deserve capital, we are launching another platform called Plum Alley Investments, which enables our members to invest on a debt and equity basis in incredibly promising and transformative female founded companies."

INDIEGOGO

I've always had a soft spot for Indiegogo. It was the platform I used to launch my Mom Gets a Business Conference Campaign. I had the pleasure of talking to Adam Chapnik, a principal of the company, whose business card title is actually "Evangelist."

Small Beginnings

Adam joined the original three founders in 2010 (Slava Rubin, Danae Ringelmann, and Eric Schell) and merged his company Distribber with Indiegogo. At the time, Indiegogo was a niche crowdfunding platform for film.

The company was formed in 2008 as a way to fund film projects. In the past six years, the platform's scope has widened to—as Adam said—"anything you can imagine." In their San Francisco headquarters, there is a giant word made of light bulbs that simply says "Empower." To the Indiegogo team, empowering means letting people create whatever they want and not curating, or creating strict guidelines for campaigns.

Adam said his team is open to everything from charitable missions to provide water to a village in Africa, to an artist who wants to make a new kind of album with a glockenspiel and a bongo. He told me that he literally cries at least once a week (tears of joy) because of the incredible impact that Indiegogo has had on individuals' lives.

What Sets Indiegogo Apart

From the beginning, Indiegogo's mission was not just for people to use the site, but also to make people feel happy. So Indiegogo named their customer support the "customer happiness" department. The company has a 97%, twenty-four hour response rate to customers.

Because Indiegogo is an inclusive platform for a variety of projects, it serves as a portal for people to be exposed to new products or ideas. If you look for a film on the site, you may also discover a new gadget, or a cause. Adam pointed out that seeing diverse projects co-exist creates a cross-pollination of things that makes each day exciting and fun for him.

The team is constantly following campaigns to see what's working for some campaigns, what's not working for other campaigns. The team shares those insights and new ideas to campaigners through the Indiegogo blog. Indiegogo also provides advice on vertical campaigns that each campaigner can learn from another.

The Future of Crowdfunding

Adam predicts that in the next year and a half, "the most famous bands on earth are going to directly distribute all of their music through crowdfunding." But he believes that crowdfunding will go beyond music. It will become a go-to marketing tool for many companies, from start-up to large brands.

The company sees crowdfunding as much more than just a fundraising opportunity. They look at it as a tool to formulate a great business plan, market your brand, connect with future customers, and conduct market research. I couldn't agree more. Think about it: you can connect with customers, get their reactions, and fine-tune your product before it hits the marketplace!

When more companies use crowdfunding as a marketing tool, they're going to realize that not only are they getting an invaluable platform for market research, they're also making money off of the campaign, essentially paying for the marketing plan and development of a product. That's going to revolutionize the way companies succeed and allow entrepreneurs to grow beyond their wildest expectations.

There are many crowdfunding site options beyond what I've offered here. A great resource to check out when researching sites is CrowdsUnite.com. CrowdsUnite is the largest user review website in the world for crowdfunding platforms. Their goal is to gather the essential information about the platforms in one location. There are filter options that allow you to search for the platforms that you qualify for then sort and compare them side-by-side.

I asked CrowdsUnite founder, Alex Feldman to send me a more comprehensive list of sites. You can do your own search here: pattylennon.com/crowdsunite Here is a list of sites that CrowdsUnite has reviewed.

KickStarter	Indiegogo	fundRazr	CrowdFunder
Ulule	Rockethub	Pozible	YouvegotFunds
Planeta	Mimoona	GigFunder	healthtechhatch
Crowdlt	PledgeMe	Rusini	BitCoinStarter
Pursuit	medstartr	Yomken	ReservoirFunds
Wahooly	PubSlush	CrowdTilt	PleaseFundUs
Haricot	Neighborly	Seed&Spark	CommunityFunded
Fundable	PeerBackers	Authr	TheHotStart
BuzzBnk	MobCaster	ZAOZAO	ScitechStarter
AppStori	FundaGeek	PPL	DedicatingDollars
SmallKnot	SpaceHive	FoodStart	DreamFundMe
GetFunded	CROFUN	MoolaHoop	WorthWild
IPledg	BloomVC	InvestYYC	FundAnything
Starteed	Indie Voices	ThrillPledge	FundMeFundYou
Smipon	Zequs	SponsorCraft	PeopleFundlt
Floosy	CrowdSupply	SonicAngel	BankToTheFuture
AppsFunder	BoomStarter		

Wow! That's a big list right? No need to get overwhelmed though. You already have everything you need to know to pick the platform that is perfect for you. Your gut and your intuition are your most valuable assets on this journey.

Using Your Intuition

When I embarked on the journey to launch a crowdfunding campaign there was absolutely no way I could have understood the powerful and transformative effect it would have on my life. In order to navigate this unknown path I read whatever I could get my hands on about the process of crowdfunding.

I also interviewed as many crowdfunders as possible. I spoke with people who have succeeded and those whom have failed. I understood that everyone who had walked this journey had a piece of the puzzle to share. Each was a teacher and I was a hungry student.

But there was a point in the journey where there were no more facts to collect and some answers just couldn't come from outside myself. At that point I needed to rely on my intuition—my gut.

The same is true for you. This book is going to take you on a step-by-step process to create a successful crowdfunding campaign. As a coach I love breaking down processes that feel big and overwhelming into small, manageable baby-steps in order to create an easier path to success. But there will be points in this journey where there is no objectively *right* answer.

In those moments you will need to look within yourself to uncover *your* right answer. How comfortable you are in following your intuitive voice will determine how easy (or difficult) this process is for you. Listening to your intuitive voice is a skill; the more you engage it the easier it becomes.

Choosing a platform is one of those points in the journey where you'll need to rely on your intuition. I can give you data. I can give you suggestions on what to look at to help you make a decision. But there is no one right answer. However, there is *your* right answer; and the great news is, that it is already inside of you.

One of the reasons that I love teaching crowdfunding so much is that there are very few rules. There just isn't enough data yet to create rules. And in environments where data is absent we are forced to create our own guidelines. As creators, we understand and honor our intuition.

We grow up learning there are right and wrong ways to do things. These rules often help us feel safe, but they also squash the natural innovator inside each of us. We need innovation right now. We need new ways of doing things. We need more people looking inside themselves for their truth—not outside to some external source of approval.

Crowdfunding gives you a training ground to harness the power of your intuitive voice and to learn that the right answer for you is always inside of you. If you are not used to listening to your intuitive voice and your own wisdom, you might need some help getting started.

You can access my free toolkit for
"Harnessing the Power of Your Intuitive Voice"
at **pattylennon.com/intuitive-toolkit**

As I mentioned earlier, I never could have dreamt up where this crowdfunding journey would take me. But every step of the way my intuitive voice continued to assure me that I was on the exact right path for me.

It guided me to uncover resources and tools that allowed me to succeed and helped me create the system to crowdfunding success that I now share with you. Your intuitive voice will guide you along your path as well. Trust and follow your intuitive voice and your success will far exceed anything your mind can conjure.

Making a Choice

Ready to start picking a platform? The first step is to learn about the options available. Take some time to visit three to ten crowdfunding sites. Write down the pros and cons of each one. Clarify what you like, what you don't like, and what you feel neutral about. Figure out what serves your needs, and what does not.

You can use the ones I've provided above or visit sites you've read about or otherwise learned about. Spend five to fifteen minutes on each site. Use the example worksheet on the following page to document one site's pros and cons.

\#___Crowdfunding Site

_____

Pros	Cons

A printable version of this worksheet is
available at **pattylennon.com/worksheets**

Now give yourself five minutes to review the pros and cons in each one. Make a quick decision and then put this decision behind you. Congratulations! You now have your crowdfunding platform picked out.

My crowdfunding platform is: _____

To become more acquainted with the site, visit it everyday for five minutes. Donate to a few campaigns ($1.00 is perfectly acceptable). This will put you in the loop of receiving updates and will invest you further in the "ecosystem" of your platform's community. Be sure to leave a note on any campaign you invest in and cheer them on. This will pay huge dividends—seen and unseen—when you launch your own campaign. This creates what I call "Crowdfunding Karma." When you offer support to fellow crowdfunders, that positive action creates a ripple effect that returns to you when you launch your own campaign.

Get a notebook or binder and keep notes on anything that jumps out at you when you are on other campaigns—likes and dislikes, general impressions, notes, or options to research more fully for your own campaign. Everything you notice is helpful and will shape your understanding of crowdfunding and what you want your own campaign to look like.

CHAPTER TWO
MARKETING STRATEGIES

Now that you have chosen your campaign platform, it's time to start planting the marketing seeds that will create your crowdfunding success.

Choosing Your Three Groups of Contributors

Hands down, the greatest benefit of crowdfunding to you is its marketing power.

I understand you are probably focused on raising capital and excited at the prospect of finally having the money you need to do your work properly. Crowdfunding is fun because it delivers cash and who doesn't love cash? However, long-term cash flow stems from effective marketing, and right now crowdfunding is the best marketing machine available to you.

Think about it. What is marketing? The Merriam Webster Dictionary defines marketing as the "action or business of promoting and selling products or services, including market research and advertising." Crowdfunding embodies the very definition of marketing!

When I work with my private business-coaching clients who are not hitting the revenue targets they dream about, almost all struggle with marketing in some form or another. And once they understand how to effectively communicate what they are doing to a wider group of people, their revenue (and joy) in their business skyrockets.

Many of us have been raised to believe that promoting ourselves is wrong. So it is not surprising that so many "good" people struggle with marketing. Promoting yourself is not about bragging. Promoting yourself is about letting people know about the amazing gifts you bring to the world, so that if they need those gifts or know someone that needs those gifts, you can reach them.

Herein lies the beauty of crowdfunding. Its very structure allows you not only to tell others what you are doing but also to help others market on your behalf. When others start marketing on your behalf your marketing power grows exponentially. For example, if you tell a friend, and she tells two friends, then they each tell their friends, **your marketing reach expands at an exponential rate**.

How would it feel to have everyone you know telling everyone they know about your product, creation, or service? Pretty awesome, right? What if you could strategically target organizations that are aligned with what you are doing and get them talking about you are doing?

This is exactly what happens with crowdfunding and here's why...

People that love and care about you want to talk about what you are doing; they just don't know how to do that. Crowdfunding gives them a simple and easy way to do it by allowing them to send their friends, family, and colleagues to a central location where your video communicates, in a compelling way, what is so special about your mission. And it does it in a non-salesy, non-cheesy way.

Crowdfunding (when it is done well) speaks to a person's heart. Traditional marketing has always been focused on grabbing people's attention and convincing them that they need what you are offering. Crowdfunding markets in a completely different way. It conveys what you plan to do and that you need support to do it. When people understand why what you are doing is so amazing, they are more likely to be a part of helping your project grow. People like to help. It feels good.

As you move through this process of creating and promoting your crowdfunding campaign, continue to remind yourself that this is a marketing process. Focus on the actions you can take that create the greatest marketing oomph.

There are also ways to strategically increase the marketing power of your campaign. The main way is to market to multiple populations. Many potential crowdfunders only focus on a single population—the people that want what they are selling, creating, inventing, etc. I call these your buyers/benefiters.

You definitely want to promote heavily to this audience, but there are other audiences that will also help get the word out. It's important not to lose sight of these populations. You should understand the motivation of these populations and market to them accordingly. These populations fall into two categories that I call **supporters/cheerleaders** and **affiliated businesses/causes.**

There are people in your life who will never want or use what you are creating but they love and care about you. You are a caring, giving person and have helped others in the past. Those people want to return the favor. I call these people your supporters/cheerleaders. This population will work hard to get the word out on your behalf because of **their emotional connection to you**.

There are also groups of people who don't necessarily know you, but have some affiliation to what you do. For these people, **your success has a ripple affect in the world that they appreciate or want to support**. I call these your affiliated businesses/causes. For example, if you are writing a book about ways to improve the American public school system, then the American Teachers Association may be a good organization to target. Or, if you have found a way to make being "green" easier for busy parents then you might target environmental groups who work to put environmentally supportive tools in the hands of parents.

As you design the marketing and communication for your crowdfunding campaign you'll want to speak to these populations differently so that they can relate to your campaign. We'll cover this later in Chapter Seven. For now, it's important to identify a few of these groups to target. This will help you develop your marketing plan.

When you start thinking about the different populations and communities that have the ability to support you, it will be easy to become overwhelmed. Know it now: you can't market to everyone. In this chapter you'll brainstorm all your options and then narrow down the list of all your potential supporters to three groups.

As I mentioned earlier, when you launch your campaign you will have an obvious focus, which is your buyer/benefiter. Your buyers/benefiters are:

- Your target customers.

- The people you are test marketing to (if applicable).

- The largest number of contributors.

It should be fairly simple to identify your buyers/benefiters. These people are the reason you do what you do. If you are building a computer app, these are the people that would use the app. If you are creating a piece of art, these are the people that would want to see that art or buy it. If you are creating an event, these are the people that would attend it.

(Note: if you are not clear who your buyer/benefiter is, this is something you'll want to get clear on before you move forward. I often help my clients with this clarity. You are welcome to email me at Patty@PattyLennon.com to see if a consult makes sense and would be helpful to you..)

My buyer/benefiter is:

_____

_____

_____

_____

Many crowdfunders keep their focus only on their buyer/benefiter—but not you! Let's spend some time brainstorming who your supporters/cheerleaders are, and who your affiliated business/causes are:

As a reminder, a supporter/cheerleader is someone who:

• Cares about you.

• Cares about your cause.

• Has a vested interest in seeing you succeed.

An affiliated business/cause is someone who:

• Has a related business or cause.

• Shares your target demographic.

• May support you simply out of good will.

• Has an aligned mission.

Knowing which supporters/cheerleaders and affiliated businesses /causes that will likely support your campaign will help you create a better marketing plan. Use the following pages to make an exhaustive list of every person, group or entity that could potentially fall into one of these groups.

If you find this process difficult, I encourage you to find a buddy with whom you can work through this process. Brainstorming on your own can be challenging. When there's an easier way (i.e. finding a buddy) choose it.

Brainstorming Worksheets

My supporters and cheerleaders are: _____

_____

_____

_____

_____

_____

_____

_____

_____

_____

_____

_____

The businesses and causes affiliated with my project are:

_____

_____

_____

_____

_____

_____

_____

_____

_____

_____

_____

_____

_____

_____

_____

_____

Printable versions of these worksheets are
available at **pattylennon.com/worksheets**

Great! Now that you have a list of everyone that may support you, let's decide which groups to focus on. You can do this in a couple of ways. My favorite method is to use your intuition. If you are using your intuition, simply scan the list of supporters/cheerleaders and affiliated businesses/ causes and pick the two that cause your or heart to leap for joy! (Note: You can refer to the intuitive voice tool on page 31 if you need help accessing your intuitive voice.) Once you pick your two, write them down.

If you are more of a cerebral gal or guy, then take the chance to look at each option and consider how strongly they align with your campaign, how much money that group likely has to contribute to your campaign, and how much influence they have on others. To me this is a very boring process and probably won't give you better information than your intuition, but if you must do the analysis you must. Spend an hour or so on each list and once the hour is up, make a decision. Write down your answers.

(Note: As we move through this material, I will encourage you to pick an amount of time and finish the action in the allotted time. This is simply to help move you along. If you find you need a bit more time, take it. Just remember that forward motion is key.)

Below, write down the three groups you will focus on marketing to during your campaign. Two of these groups should be from your list of supporters/cheerleaders and affiliated businesses/causes. The third group should be your buyers/benefiters.

The 3 Groups I will focus on marketing to during my campaign are:

1. _____

2. _____

3. _____

(It is possible that two of your three groups come from one worksheet, either from the affiliated businesses/causes worksheet or from the supporters/cheerleaders worksheet. This is normal.)

Now we want to decide where your potential contributors and supporters are hanging out so you can start spending time with them.

We are going to create what I call your "likeability campaign." Your likeability campaign is the work you will do prior to launching your crowdfunding campaign to connect with your potential contributors and supporters. Your goal is to become more likeable. Being likable isn't something you can fake. Help others. Give them information or support. Do it over time. When you need it they'll be there for you.

Use the following sample worksheet to uncover the information you'll need to launch your likeability campaign. Complete three worksheets—one for each of the three contributor groups you noted above.

Places my contributor group spends time:

Social Media: _____

_____

_____

_____

_____

In Person: _____

_____

_____

_____

_____

On Blogs: _____

_____

_____

_____

_____

Other: _____

_____

_____

_____

_____

_____

A printable version of this worksheet is
available at **pattylennon.com/worksheets**

Woohoo! You now have the foundation for you likeability
campaign. Let's craft your likeability campaign and determine how you can show up in key places for your potential
contributors and supporters.

Showing Up—the Key to Being Likeable

SOCIAL MEDIA

The way to "show up" on social media is to be present on
the social media platforms that your potential contributors
and supporters visit most often. You may find that your
three groups spend time on multiple social media platforms. Just know that you can't be everywhere all the time

so don't try to be—pick one or two social platforms (e.g. Twitter, Facebook, LinkedIn, Pinterest, etc.) and develop a strong presence there.

While you are there, show appreciation for your potential contributors and supporters. Do this by retweeting, sharing, re-pinning, and liking whatever it is that you like. It's important to be authentic in this process; don't do anything that doesn't feel true to you. (We'll discuss more about how to harness the power of each of these social media platforms in Chapter Seven.)

Spend fifteen to twenty minutes a day on the social media outlet you decide to focus on. If you are focusing on two, spend twenty to thirty minutes total on both. You can get sucked into the black hole of social media very easily, so be sure to set a timer and stop when your time is up!

One social media platform I will focus on is:_____

A second social media platform is (if applicable): _____

Blogs

Bloggers are quite influential to their loyal readers. Having the support of a blogger that influences your audience of potential contributors and supporters is incredibly valuable when you are crowdfunding.

That blogger might be willing to run a guest blog post you write or mention you and your campaign in a blog while your campaign is live. They will do this if they know you and like you. The best way to get known is to "show up" on the blog.

How to "Show Up" on Blogs

Earlier in the chapter you made a list of the blogs your potential contributors and supporters read. Here are some things you can do to create a greater presence on those blogs:

- Begin to read these blogs.

- Leave comments and share these blogs on social media.

- When you share the blogs, tag the blogger so they see the support you are giving them and start to recognize your name and social media handles.

We'll talk more about how to harness the power of influential bloggers in Chapter Seven but for now, start being friendly to your targeted bloggers. I recommend following ten blogs. Review the worksheets you just completed. Complete the following worksheet with blogs relevant to your contributors.

Choose five blogs where your primary contributor (your buyer/benefiter) spends time.

1. _____

2. _____

3. _____

4. _____

5. _____

Choose five additional blogs where your two additional contributor and supporter groups spend time. This would be the groups you noted on page 44.

6. _____

7. _____

8. _____

9. _____

10. _____

A printable version of this worksheet is available at **pattylennon.com/worksheets**

Most blogs have a service that allows you to receive automated updates when a new blog is posted through an RSS feed. If the blogs you're focusing on don't, you may need to put a reminder on your calendar to check each week. Spend fifteen minutes two to three times a week reading, commenting, and sharing these blogs.

In-Person/Power Networking

The way you "show up" in person is probably obvious—you physically show up. Review your worksheets and determine where your potential contributors are, and where you can reasonably join them in person. Then go there. This may be networking groups, conferences, social groups, your children's school, etc. When you are there, be prepared to speak about your upcoming campaign and collect the names of people interested in supporting you.

How much time you spend on in-person networking is really dependent on your personal situation. The more time you spend networking, the better—so do the best you can to get out and about. Remember, networking isn't just benefiting your future campaign—networking is a powerful way to drive sales today!

In order to make the most of in-person networking I recommend creating a business card specifically for this purpose. On your new business card you should have the following information:

- A visual element representing your campaign (e.g. picture, or logo)

- Your name

- Your custom domain name*

- Your email address

- A blank side to write notes or other information

You can purchase inexpensive business cards at sites like:

- vistaprint.com

- uprinting.com

- zazzle.com

*Your Custom Domain Name

A custom domain name is your springboard for marketing and sales. Choose a domain name that is easy to remember, easy to say, easy to spell, and of course, available. For example, when I launched the Mom Gets a Business Conference® Campaign, my custom domain name was supportmombiz.com

You can reserve a custom domain name at sites like:

- godaddy.com

- 1and1.com

- domainname.com

Once you have the domain name, set up a redirect to your website page that describes what you will be crowdfunding (the product, event, business, etc.) If you already have a website, you can simply point it there. If you don't, you will want to put up a single website page giving a brief description of what you are planning to fund, and when the campaign will launch. Once your crowdfunding campaign goes live, you will want to immediately point the custom domain name to the campaign URL.

In my case, I redirected supportmombiz.com to the conference website until my crowdfunding campaign went live. The morning it went live, I redirected supportmombiz.com to the Indiegogo site for my crowdfunding campaign. If you do not know how to redirect your domain name to another URL (also called masking), the service you use to reserve the domain name will be able to walk you through this process.

This may seem like a lot of work, but it will pay huge dividends as you network in person. It gives you an easy way to send people to your campaign once it goes live because you are able to speak the URL or domain name in conversation. The URL you get from your crowdfunding will be a series of letters or numbers that are not easily spoken or recalled.

Also, when you have a custom domain name you have control over what people are viewing. So when someone visits you via that custom domain they will be led to wherever you decide to redirect that custom domain. If your campaign is live you should have the custom domain redirected to the campaign. The day your campaign ends you can redirect this custom domain back to your product or promotional web page.

Likewise when you are handing out business cards before your campaign goes live, you can redirect the custom domain featured on the business card to your product or promotional web page.

By using a custom domain you are able to give out the same web address before, during, and after your campaign. This ensures that potential contributors and supporters don't get confused and are always looking where you want them to be looking. You have full control over what part of your project potential contributors get to see.

Build Your List

As you network, you will also want to collect the names of the people who are willing to support your campaign in a systemized way. You can create something as simple as an excel spreadsheet or use a more advanced approach like an email management system such as MailChimp or Constant Contact.

If you are using an email management system for your business already, you can simply set up a separate list for your campaign supporters.

If you would like to use an email management system and haven't done so in the past, there are many options.

MailChimp is free, and can be found at mailchimp.com.

Constant Contact has great customer service. I'm an affiliate of Constant Contact, so if you do decide to go with them I'd love for you to use my affiliate link.

Please Use my Constant Contact affiliate link:
pattylennon.com/constant-contact

There are many more services that provide email management, so if you don't like either of these, you can reach out to your network or search on Google and you'll find plenty of recommendations.

Every email management service has training that will walk you through how to optimize the service. If you do decide to use an email management system, I strongly recommend adding an "opt-in" box to your website which prompts people to give you their information if they want to be updated about your campaign.

As you collect names and emails of people that want to be updated when your campaign goes live, you will be able to enter these directly into your email management system. Each system differs, so please use your email management's training and customer service to support you in doing this.

If you are working with one of our certified consultants on your campaign they'll also be able to provide you personalized assistance with this.

For a list of certified Crowdfund with Ease™ consultants, visit: **pattylennon.com/services**

Start building your contact list today. I'll get you started. Here is my information, which you can add to the list of people supporting your campaign:

Name: Patty Lennon

Email: Patty@PattyLennon.com

Please be sure to email me in advance that you are adding me to your list, so I know to look for updates to your campaign! That concludes your homework for the second chapter. This is a tremendous amount of work. Be proud of yourself!

Recap of your Likeability Campaign

- Fifteen to thirty minutes on social media daily

- Fifteen minutes on a few of your ten targeted blogs, two to three times per week

- In person networking as often as possible.

You've done a great job. Now go out there and be likeable!

CHAPTER THREE
CREATING YOUR PITCH VIDEO

Until now you have been laying the groundwork to create a group of supporters and contributors for your campaign page when it goes live. Now we are going to focus on the work that turns potential contributors who visit your campaign into actual contributors who donate to your campaign.

The heart and soul of your campaign is your **pitch video**. It sets the tone of your campaign, conveys your message, and is the key to effectively marketing your campaign. Although a pitch video is not required on some crowdfunding platforms, campaigns with pitch videos are far more successful than those without. A statistic Indiegogo offered in 2011 was that: campaigns with a pitch video raised 114% more than those without. I expect that number is much higher now, as the total number of campaigns has grown.

Most potential contributors will decide whether to contribute to your campaign based solely on what they see in your pitch video. A great pitch video converts unsure, potential contributors to money-offering supporters.

In this chapter we'll cover everything you need to know to create a successful pitch video.

The key to driving viewers and donations to your crowdfunding campaign is in engaging the minds and hearts of potential contributors. You do this by following what I call the T.L.C. system of pitching.

T—**Touch** their heart and make them **think**

L—Make them **laugh**

C—Make them **care**; bonus points for making them **cry**

Take some time to watch at least ten videos of crowdfunding campaigns on the platform you chose on page 34. Take note of what you like and don't like. Which campaigns engage your heart and mind? If you've donated to campaigns in the past (and please tell me you've donated to campaigns in the past—crowdfunding karma, remember?) go back and watch the associated videos. At one time these videos moved you to support a certain cause and campaign, and that is a powerful trait.

Note to the camera shy: If you don't love being in front of the camera it may be tempting to avoid the spotlight in your video pitch. Potential contributors should be able to connect with YOU through the video. As you take notes on other videos, pay attention to how important your connection to the crowdfunder is in your decision to contribute. You'll see the critical role they play in connecting you to their cause. And maybe you'll be inspired when it's time for you to be in front of the camera.

No two people or pitches are alike. You may love something that someone else despises. Your job in creating a pitch video is not to create something that everyone loves—it is to create something that *your* people love and can relate to.

As you watch your ten videos, don't worry about what other people like or don't like. Feel it for yourself, because you are the best representation of the people you'll be reaching out to as donors.

On the following worksheets, take note of where each pitch video you watch uses T.L.C. Also notice what other factors work for, or against, the campaign. Anything you notice— good or bad—will help you create a better pitch.

Some additional components to look for are:

- Lighting

- Sound quality

- Speaker's pitch

- Hand gestures

- Background

- Music

Video #_____ Notes

URL: _____

Ways it **touched** my heart and made me **think:** _____

_____

_____

_____

_____

_____

_____

Ways it made me **laugh:** _____

_____

_____

_____

_____

_____

_____

Ways it made me **care** or **cry:** _____

_____

_____

_____

_____

_____

_____

Other observations: _____

_____

_____

_____

_____

_____

_____

_____

A printable version of this worksheet is available at **pattylennon.com/worksheets**

Once you've had a chance to review ten other campaigns videos, your vision for your pitch video will be much clearer. No matter what you observed, key components in the videos probably ignited whatever connections you forged to the campaigns.

People crave connection—connection to individuals and to the world at large. When you present a video pitch that causes people to feel like part of something greater than themselves, they will support you. The easiest way to do this is to understand and clarify *why* you are embarking on this campaign. In this chapter we will focus on helping you do just that!

If you've ever seen Simon Sinek's TED Talk on *How Great Leaders Inspire Action*, then you are already familiar with the value of *why*. Before you go any further, please watch Sinek's talk here: pattylennon.com/simon-sinek-ted. (If you've never seen this TED Talk, get ready to be inspired!)

Pay special attention around the 3:30 mark. Mr. Sinek describes the way most companies sell, as opposed to the way truly extraordinary companies sell. Think about the way you engage customers—where are you speaking from—the *what* or the *why*? Note anything (and I mean anything) that grasps your attention while watching this talk—all of it's valuable!

Fill out the below worksheet about Simon Sinek's talk.

Notes on Simon Sinek's TED Talk,
How Great Leaders Inspire Action

Inspirations, Realizations, Awarenesses, Aha! Moments:

_____

_____

_____

_____

_____

_____

_____

_____

_____

_____

_____

_____

_____

A printable version of this worksheet is
available at **pattylennon.com/worksheets**

Your Big Why

It's time to get down to why you are doing what you are doing—in this crowdfunding campaign and in life. This is heavy stuff, I know, but it's important. The closer you get to the center of the circle of *why*, the more easily money will flow to your campaign.

Ideally, whatever you are crowdfunding is directly linked to your greater mission on this earth. When one human being speaks to another about her or his purpose or mission, this first person naturally engages others. Have you ever watched someone speak about a topic you would normally find utterly disinteresting, but because of that person's passion you find yourself engaged?

Many people are numb right now. They are overworked and exhausted. Life is moving at a frenetic pace, and many are having a hard time keeping up. As a result, they shut down. They numb themselves with TV, drugs, alcohol, food, and sex. They numb themselves to escape. They really want to feel alive, to slow down, and to feel connected to other human beings. If you make a person feel connected to you—if you remind them what passion looks like—they will help you.

Your *Big Why* is your passion, so let's get to it. Using the following worksheet, let's uncover your *Big Why*. Using a very simple set of questions, allow yourself to dig deep, and get to the juicy core of it!

Big Why

Why this crowdfunding campaign?

_____

_____

_____

_____

_____

So What? _____

_____

_____

_____

_____

So What? _____

_____

_____

_____

_____

So What? _____

_____

_____

_____

_____

So What? _____

_____

_____

_____

_____

_____

A printable version of this worksheet is available at pattylennon.com/worksheets

Now that you are clear on your *Big Why,* let's get down to the business of creating a video that showcases your reason for living—I mean your reason for crowdfunding.

Video Production

If you have the budget, I strongly recommend hiring a video production team. Prior to filming my pitch video, I never could have imagined how much work it is to technically produce a high-quality video. The price tag can seem steep, (you can expect to pay anywhere from $1,500-$4,000 for a high quality, fully-edited pitch video) but with the right team it is money well spent.

Video Production Team

When considering a video production team be sure to do the following:

- Obtain three recommendations from previous customers. Speak with the customers directly. In your conversation ask them about professionalism, ability to reach deadlines, ease of communication, quality of end product, and whether any reshoots were required and, if so, why.

- Review three to five samples of the team's work.

- If the company has multiple team members, ensure the recommendations and samples are a direct reflection of the team you'll be working with.

- Get a signed contract detailing exactly what's covered with your fee, your payment schedule, and deliverable dates.

Making the Most of Your Money

The majority of work that goes into producing a pitch video is in the scripting and filming of the video. If you plan it well, you can use this time to create not one, but three videos! I recommend brainstorming with your video production team on creating the following:

- Crowdfunding Pitch Video (ideally two minutes or less).

- Sizzle reel for your product, event, or project website (2:30-3:00 minutes).

- Short commercial for your project to use when promoting to a potential sponsor or on social media (thirty seconds).

These three videos can use the same footage, so it's just a matter of some additional editing to create the final three cuts. You'll want your video team to let you know up front what the total quote will be with this additional editing. The only difference between the pitch video and sizzle reel is that you will swap out the call-to-action at the end of the video and add in a bit more of the "what" for the sizzle reel.

Script Writing

Once you have your production team in place you'll want to script your pitch video. If you are unable to budget for a production team, you still need to create a script. If you are working with a team they will help you through this process.

Scripting Without a Team

If you are scripting on your own, here's a great article I found on ehow.com on how to write a basic script:

pattylennon.com/write-video-script

I also loved some of the points in this section of Go Animate:

pattylennon.com/storyboard-tips. Just keep in mind that they are writing primarily for someone involved in a commercial venture who will be focused on the *what* more than the *why*.

If you're writing your script without a video production team, at the very least you should get the help of some friends or colleagues so you can bounce ideas off them.

Check out local high school and college media departments for resources, as well. They can be a great source of budget-friendly help.

Questions to answer in your script

A simple way to structure a script is to list out questions and answers. Most of the questions should allow you to expand on your *Big Why*. Some other questions to consider are:

- Who are you?

- What is your project?

- How is your background relevant to this project?

- Why should a viewer trust you?

- What's so special about your project?

- How will this project change the world (whatever size world that is)?

- What does the project look like?

- How long will it take to complete the project? (Only include this if the timeline is relevant to the viability of the project).

- How much backing do you need to complete the project?

- How will you use the money? (Give an overview in the video. Details can go in the written description).

- What rewards are you offering? (Include these only if they tie into the *why*. Keep the details high-level)

- What will you do if you get more money than you are asking for? (This isn't absolutely necessary but if you are looking for a small dollar amount in the hopes of overfunding, you'll want to explain that here).

Have someone stand behind the cameraperson and prompt you with the questions as you answer them into the camera. The actual recorded questions should not be used in the videos. Be sure to restate the question in your answer—so the viewer has a context to the prompted question. This will create the best production flow.

For instance, if the question is "Why do you feel compelled to invent a solution for brushing teeth with your feet?" then your answer might look like this: "The reason I am compelled to invent a solution for brushing teeth with my feet is ..."

In this chapter's DIY Filming section I'll give you some additional shortcuts for creating powerful scripts.

BRoll & Voiceovers

B-roll is supplemental or alternate footage intercut with the main shot in an interview or documentary. If you have a production team, they'll talk you through what type of b-roll shots you should seek. If you're doing this on your own, you'll want to think this through. These are the images that will support your greater mission.

You can shoot the b-roll by yourself or purchase stock video if it works for the feel of your pitch. Here is an article I found that lists a number of free stock video sites:

pattylennon.com/stock-video. You can also simply search Google for "stock video" to find a host of other options.

No matter whom you are helping (the homeless, moms, overworked execs, etc.), your video will be more powerful if you give a face to the population or problem. B-roll is a great way to do this. It also allows you to change up the content more easily if you find there is a point you missed that you want cut in. With b-roll you can record a voiceover and have that cut in without having to reshoot. Voiceovers are typically recorded with a video camera, but you can use a high quality microphone and your computer to do this as well.

Brainstorm some b-roll shots you'd love to have: _____

_____

_____

_____

_____

_____

Testimonials

Testimonials are extremely useful because they personalize your message from an objective standpoint and emphasize the power of your solution. It would be ideal to incorporate a few ten-fifteen second testimonials

In Chapter Five we'll brainstorm some people who can give you testimonials but if anyone comes to mind right now jot their names down here: _____

_____

_____

_____

_____

Blane Friest, video producer and founder of DDM Productions, offers this feedback on capturing testimonials:

Tips for Capturing Testimonials
Blane Friest

The testimonial when captured and used properly can be the most effective tool for growing a vibrant community and turning viewers into contributors.

So, I hereby introduce you to TAPS, an acronym I've developed to help people remember the important elements of a testimonial whether written or video.

Timing. Like just about everything else in the world, timing is everything. It's of paramount importance that you ask for or offer the testimonial when you are most emotionally connected to the subject. And keep it short!

Authentic. This is the most important of the four pieces. In this age of information overload, we as a culture really have developed a very sensitive nose for bull$#!t. If the person offering a testimonial is not coming from her heart, speaking her truth, whatever that may be, people will know. Using that testimonial in your pitch video will be doing more damage than good.

Pain. A person must be in great pain to give a good testimonial. I suggest striking a thumb (on the non-dominant hand, preferably) with a hammer or some other steel ended implement. Kidding...BUT for a testimonial to be truly effective, the kind that really does turn potential contributors into actual contributors, the person offering the testimonial must clearly state the pain the person was in prior to receiving the product, service, etc.

Story. We have the opportunity to bring technology full circle and use it to ACTUALLY connect with real humans. What really gets and keeps attention, what makes a real impression, is a story. A story told from the heart and with integrity. This is where the pain in the previous step gets resolved and the viewer really GETS how important the work of the subject of the testimonial really is.

So, there it is. It takes practice to get comfortable both asking for and giving testimonials.

I suggest that you pull out your smart phone right now, start the video recorder, and tell someone about the great service you got at, say, the donut counter this morning. Get the practice. If you're really interested in experiencing the power of a testimonial first hand, make the effort to find out who the manager is for that guy from the donut counter and email the manager your testimonial.

Watch the impact that creates! And with testimonials—like love—the more you give, the more you get!

DIY Filming

If it is at all possible to invest in professional help with your video I strongly recommend you do so. However, if budgeting requires that you go it alone I asked Blane to give you some help in making your pitch video the best it can possible be. Here are Blane Friest's tips for DIY filming.

Tips for DIY Filming
Blane Friest

I'm not going to bore you with all the statistics that indicate how powerful and effective video is in connecting with your audience and your potential contributors. You already know you need a video. In fact, some crowdfunding sites now REQUIRE a video for campaigns.

Face it people, you are trying to sell something. Whether it's an idea, a product, or service that you're funding—you're selling. You're actually always selling, whether it's to that handsome guy you want to take you to ice cream, or your boss you're convincing you deserve to take home another $50 a week. You're always selling. And there's nothing wrong with that.

I believe the best way to create sales is to present yourself and your product or project authentically and with integrity. After over 30+ years in the performing arts and having worked in and out of Wall Street, I have come to the conclusion that storytelling through video is the most efficient and effective way to connect with large numbers of the right people—the people who will actually become contributing members of your thriving community. As crowdfunders, you've made a choice. That choice is: the best way to get your "stuff" out there is by building community.

Although it would be impossible for me to share everything I know in a few short pages, I will cover the key areas of production when doing your own video production: mindset, scripting, lighting, and sound.

Mindset

A few words on mindset before we go further: you've heard me mention the words 'authenticity' and 'integrity' already, and you'll hear them from me over and over. There are two reasons why I feel authenticity is the key to being successful with your video.

1. With so much crap out there on the web, our media meters are fully tuned to heightened 'BS' sensitivity; your audience (the people you want in your community) are going to sense it if it's there. More accurately, they'll feel it—and it's as easy as *click*, they're gone. When you are authentic and operate with integrity, people will stay and listen.

2. This one may be even more important...When you are authentic you are telling *your* story. It is you and it's the reason you've done all the work and taken all that risk to create something new to bring to the world. Telling *your* story keeps *you* interested. It keeps you engaged AND it makes the process way more fun for you and your team!

So, what happens to you when you sit down to shoot some video? If you're like most people, you either get really weird and disconnected from yourself, (and your message) or you just freeze. This isn't unusual at all. The number one fear is public speaking and this 'weirdness' is simply the manifestation of that fear on video.

In fact, I used to freeze up in front of the camera, as well. That changed when I was able to reawaken my inner actor. Now I really do look forward to getting in front of the camera and talking with you. That has given me tremendous freedom. I want that same freedom and power for you!

So how do you get past this fear? It's a shift in mindset. I have two fairly simple ways I get my clients in the mindset to shoot effective video.

The first is to clearly identify the person you're talking to. This might sound a little odd since you are trying to connect with a whole lot of folks to fund your project. The thing is, that when you are speaking to that one person, you are speaking your authentic truth from your heart. The person doesn't actually have to exist in real life; you just need to imagine them. In the case of your pitch video you want to picture your ideal buyer/benefiter.

Describe this one person in as much detail as you can. Fill in all the particulars and life experiences of your target contributor or your buyer/benefiter. Be thorough. Even include things like favorite color, best friend in third grade, or favorite ice cream. Do what you need to do to make this person into a real fully fleshed-out person.

This is the person you envision every time you talk into a camera. Heck, once you've created this person, go on the

Internet and find a picture that fits that person; print it out so you can quickly snap into a conversation with this person.

When I work with clients privately we do this work together. So if you are stuck, find a partner to work with you on this.

Scripting

The second way to shift your mindset is to clarify your message. Write your manifesto. This process will also give you the structure for your script. The manifesto I help people with has just a few simple steps but it's powerful. When you're clear what your purpose is, then that will keep you connected with your heart and your passion; and, your purpose will come through loud and clear. Each of these five parts should have ideally two, but no more than three answers. When answering, be simple, clear and direct.

1. Who am I? Two-three things stated as, "I am ..."

2. Who are you (target contributor)? Stated as, "You are..."

For example, if I were doing a crowdfunding campaign to fund my Video Marketing Mastery System I would answer with this:

You are an entrepreneur with an incredible, world changing product, service or idea that you just can't get to the right people. You're frustrated and exhausted, working so hard to perfect your product that you are

*completely overwhelmed with the idea of marketing and
selling it. You need an easy, and more importantly FUN,
way to get your message to the people whose lives would
be transformed if they could just find you.*

3. Why are you doing this? Or more accurately, what
pain point exists in the world that you can fix?
What made you take the risk to begin this project?
This is where you get connected with your story and
your passion.

What pain can your ideal contributor connect to? Again,
the clearer you are, the more effective your pitch will be. I
personally have a particularly difficult time with this part.
I come from a long line of Norwegian gentleman bachelor
farmers; we never admit our own pain, and would **never**
admit seeing the pain of another. Face it, you started your
project because of some kind of pain you were experiencing. Unless you clearly connect to the pain of your contributors, you're going to lose them.

4. What problem do I solve? Yay! Now we get to have
some fun. Write two to three short, direct sentences
telling your person *why* your project is the best solution to the problem at hand.

And to wrap up your script add...

5. Call to action. You've touched their hearts. Now
what? Be clear about what you want your contributor to do next. According to Patty, our crowdfunding

maven, the call to action for a crowdfunding campaign is:

- Contribute to the campaign

- Share the campaign with friends and family

- Leave a supportive comment

Once you have your answers you have your manifesto. Your manifesto gives you the basis for your script. When I work with clients we create this manifesto together, then spend some time telling a bit more of the story, drop in some testimonials, and we have a script. It's extremely powerful and effective.

Once we have a script, we produce the video. Will this work for your crowdfunding video? Absolutely! Can you do it yourself? A resounding YES!

Do you want to do it yourself? That is a question you need to answer for yourself. You can determine your answer by responding to a couple of questions.

- Do you have the technical expertise to shoot and edit your video (you probably have nearly all the equipment and software you need)?

- Do you have the time (and team) to be a producer of your product AND your marketing video?

If the answers are "yes!" here are some things you want to keep in mind when shooting your own videos.

- It's all about the lighting and sound.

- It's all about the lighting. (I started out in this business as a lighting designer).

- It's also all about the sound.

Lighting and Sound

It doesn't matter how amazing your idea is or that your story is the most compelling thing since the Duck Dynasty controversy—if your audience can't tell what they're looking at, and is straining to understand what you're saying, you've lost them. Period.

I have a ton of stories (and a bunch of video examples on my site) of people spending a time and energy to shoot video that ends up being useless.

I'm going to assume that you're using one of the amazing cameras on your iPhone (4s or better), iPad, or other similar device that will shoot high-definition video (at least 720p). I prefer shooting everything in 1080p but that makes for awfully large files and while it looks better on a computer screen, 720p is just fine.

Lighting

Probably the single most important thing to know about lighting is that your subject needs to be more brightly lit than the background. I've seen so many videos done where the speaker is sitting in front of a window on a bright sunshiny day and the subject speaking is nothing but a shadowed outline because the window is brighter than her face!

When shooting you will want to use three-point lighting (detailed below), which is the standard, especially if you're shooting indoors. Here's a link to an affordable kit you can get from Amazon (pattylennon.com/lighting-kit). It has a boom stand for your hair light and two for key and fill lights. I also have purchased three additional bulbs and clip-on work lights that I use for additional fill (pattylennon.com/studio-light-bulb and pattylennon.com/clamp-light).

I wouldn't recommend trying to shoot in front of a green screen and using a chroma key. It's difficult to make that kind of filming look professional. What I've done is paint a wall in my living room flat white and it works great for the infinite white look (the look Apple has made so popular in its TV commercials).

The three points of three-point lighting are as follows:

1. Key:

Key light is the primary light for your subject. Ideally, it's going to be 45 degrees above and 45 degrees to the side of your subject's face. Start there, but keep in mind this is a guideline and not a hard and fast rule. Take a short test shot or video to see how it's going to look when recorded.

Your primary light is going to be a little brighter than the fill, which is your secondary light. A few shadows and a few hotspots (for instance, a little bright spot on your cheek) are natural. When there are no shadows or hotspots the subject looks flat and 2D. Take a look at someone outdoors sometime. The sun is the key-light. It creates bright spots and shadows. Your key-light plays the part of the sun.

2. Fill:

Your secondary light is the fill. The key light *will* create shadows. The purpose of the fill—or secondary light—is to make the shadows less severe. Again, start at 45 degrees up and 45 degrees to the side, and adjust until you get something that looks good to you. I will often keep the key at closer to 45° and 45° and position the fill at slightly more acute angles.

3. Top or Hair Light:

This is exactly what it sounds like. This is the light that falls at the top of the head. The purpose of this light is to create separation of your subject from the background. I generally don't use color for these lights, but when watching live TV you will often see a white or colored light on the head and shoulders of the person on camera.

NOTE: The separation is what's important, not necessarily the origin of the light. If you don't have any way to get a light overhead, a light as high as you can get it from each side will work just fine for these purposes. Just make sure you are taking test shots so you are confident that you'll like the finished product before you take all the time to shoot.

Do you have to buy a professional light kit to shoot these? No. Last night I shot a video for a friend on the fly in her living room using my iPhone (on a mini tripod which I always carry with me...geek that I am), two desk lamps, the overhead fixture, and a floor lamp with it's shade off. The video ended up being pretty darn good.

If you're going to do something like this, there are a couple of things I want you to keep in mind. The first is that all the lights need to have the same kind of bulb in them so the color of the light is consistent for the shoot. Take a look at the difference between a fluorescent, LED, and an old school incandescent light bulb sometime. Each has a completely different color and quality of light. In fact, try to avoid shooting under fluorescents all together unless they're professional color balanced bulbs with the color temperature clearly marked on them. I can't get into more detail about this here. That's a whole other book—Lighting 201.

One final comment about lighting—sometimes it's great and completely relevant to shoot outdoors. For these shoots, stay out of direct sunlight; it's just too bright. Shooting on a sunny day is good, but you should find somewhere the sunlight is diffused (under a tree) or reflected onto something (make sure the reflector is not too colorful or shiny to avoid glare). If you're outdoors, you have the added challenge of sound issues though, which leads me to my next topic.

Sound

Essentially the same rules for lighting apply to sound. Keep your environment in mind. Make sure the subject is louder and more intelligible than the surrounding area. This can be done in a number of ways, but remember that test shots are important to ensure you don't waste an entire afternoon shooting something that won't be usable. You **don't** want to try to overdub and synch voiceovers unless you're trying to do your own remake of Woody Allen's "What's up, Tiger Lily" (which is hilarious, by the way). Leave that for the pros.

This is where you might want to make a small investment in an external microphone. There are a number of boom/ directional microphones in the hundred-dollar range that you can use with an iPod or iPad. These are useful if you're shooting in an environment where you don't have the ability to create silence. There are also a couple of decent clip on mic options in the twenty-five to forty dollar range that do the trick. You can buy these mics from Amazon. com at pattylennon.com/lavelier-mic.

They're not great, but are much more isolating than the mic on any smartphone. So they're beneficial if you're going to shoot in public areas or get interviews and/or testimonials. When I shoot many of my selfie "on-the-spot" videos, I usually just use the mic on the ear-buds that came with my iPhone. I jerry-rigged a lapel clip to the buds and tuck them into my shirt. It works just fine. Keep in mind these mics are omnidirectional (i.e. they pick up pretty much every sound around) so you want to be in a somewhat controlled environment. But this is just another example of something you probably already have that will work just fine with some practice and effort.

Do some Googling and make sure that the mic you're buying will work with your phone. You probably need a powered mic if you're using your mobile device. With the new iPhone you may need an adapter. Try kVconnection; it is a good resource to find all kinds of audio adapters. (pattylennon.com/iphone-adapters)

Once you have your equipment it's time to schedule your day of filming.

Schedule Your Day of Filming

Have your schedule laid out for your day of filming. Do not wing it. That is all I'll say. There is no "right" way to schedule—just know when and where everything needs to take place.

Prep Yourself

Prior to shooting, be sure to drink plenty of water, avoid alcohol and salt, get a moderate amount of movement/exercise, and get a good night's sleep.

Keep Control of Your Script and Editing

A great production team will be as excited about your mission or campaign as you are. I had this happen with me, and it was a pleasure to have that enthusiasm on my side. However, the downside to an enthusiastic team is they'll want to convey all your great points through their favorite medium—video. You can't convey *everything* in video; your video will be too long.

You are the leader. You are in charge! You must set the vision and drive the end product. If your production team is used to doing sizzle reels for commercial ventures, they may not be as sensitive to the target length (less than two minutes) or they may not be able to focus on the "why" over the "what." You'll need to push back when they think of going long or having too much "what."

Own Your Stuff!

When producing any video, be sure you have the rights to anything you use to produce your video—music, images, testimonials, etc. If someone is giving you any of these, get a contract in writing that states your right to use these items without charge.

Have Fun!

Most importantly, have fun with this! Yes, it is a big endeavor, but it is also your work. When your soul is playing in the field of your purpose, its natural state is play! Have a sense of humor. Find pleasure in the small acts of magic that happen throughout your film creation. Love your life! This makes the best video, anyway.

CHAPTER FOUR
STRUCTURING YOUR FUNDING

Fixed vs. Flexible Funding

Many potential crowdfunders struggle with the decision of choosing a flexible funding structure or a fixed (all-or-nothing) funding structure. There are very few times when flexible funding makes sense. From a marketing perspective, fixed funding campaigns are far more effective in encouraging donations. Here is what Salvador Briggman of CrowdCrux offered on this:

Choosing a Funding Style

SALVADOR BRIGGMAN

If you're thinking of starting a crowdfunding campaign, you may have come across the two phrases "all-or-nothing" and "flexible funding."

When fundraising for an all-or-nothing crowdfunding campaign, you will only receive the pledges that you have accumulated throughout the duration of the campaign **if** you meet your fundraising goal before the clock winds down.

For example, if you have a fundraising goal of $10,000 and have only raised $9,000 by the end of your 30-day campaign, you will not receive any funds and your backers will not have their credit cards charged.

When fundraising for a flexible funding campaign, you will receive the pledges that you have accumulated throughout the duration of the campaign even if you do not meet your fundraising goal.

For example, if you raise $4,000 in 30 days with a $5,000 goal, you would still be allowed to keep the $4,000 and your backers' credit cards would be charged.

How does your choice impact the fundraising process?

Fees

Often times, if you choose to run a flexible funding campaign over an all-or-nothing campaign, you will end up paying higher platform fees. For example, if you were to launch a flexible funding campaign on Indiegogo you would end up paying a 9% fee of funds raised if you didn't meet your goal. However, you would pay the standard 4% fee if you did meet your goal.

According to Indiegogo, this "encourages people to set reasonable goals and promote their campaigns." Essentially, it is more costly if you fail with a flexible funding campaign, but at least you will receive funds for your project.

Incentive

Arguably, when you are running an all-or-nothing crowd-funding campaign, you are naturally motivated to work harder to reach your fundraising goal. If you don't work hard to drive traffic to the page and convince backers that you have a worthwhile project, then you won't receive any funds at all for your endeavor, even if you've managed to attract some backers.

If you are working with a team, this can be a powerful motivator. It encourages your team members to put forth full effort throughout the duration of the campaign so that their efforts are not in vain.

Selling Point

When convincing friends, family members, and strangers to back your dream, selecting an all-or-nothing campaign gives you one important selling point. Your backers' credit cards will not be charged unless you reach your fundraising goal.

This feature adds an element of insurance for your contributors. They are not just donating money or giving money away to your pet project. You will only receive their funds if you secure pledges sufficient to meet your goal and make your dream a reality. It's not charity. It's an investment.

Project Completion

The best crowdfunding projects are transparent and create a sense of community around the mission or goal. It's difficult to maintain that community if you end up shipping your rewards extremely late. You may also receive complaints from backers and angry comments on your project.

It might seem like a nice deal to receive some funds for your project via flexible funding, but if these funds don't allow you to follow through with all of your backer rewards, or prohibit you from distributing copies of the product, then it could be some time before your supporters are compensated for their financial contributions.

Sal's Recommendation

If distributing your rewards (oftentimes a version of the product) is dependent on receiving enough funds to actually produce the product, then I'd recommend going with an all-or-nothing campaign.

If your project is more cause-related or donation-based, then a flexible funding campaign may be more appropriate because it ensures that you will, at least, receive some funds to use toward your cause.

I think that creators might underestimate the impact that an all-or-nothing campaign can have on the morale of your team or backers.

For example, imagine you are $3,000 away from your goal in an all-or-nothing campaign. You communicate to your supports that if a certain percentage of them raised their contribution by a certain amount, the project would become a reality. Your supporters are much more likely to raise their pledge amount in this case, than if you were doing a flexible funding campaign. With a flexible funding campaign you would receive funds regardless of whether or not you reached your fundraising goal.

Once you have determined whether you are doing an "all-or-nothing" or flexible funding campaign it is time to determine your funding goal.

Calculating Your Funding Goal

Calculating your funding goal is absolutely an art, and never an exact science. No two contributors (or their social connections) look the same. Regardless, everyone likes to have an equation when it comes to something like calculating your funding goal, so here is the one I use with my private clients. I want to stress that I make no guarantees about the accuracy of this number—your understanding of your circle has a lot to do with whether this number works or not. So without further ado, here is the equation and explanation.

Mentally review the list of people you can reasonably expect to contribute to your campaign. Guesstimate what their average funding amount will be. Multiply the funding amount by the number of people, and that will give you

40% of your goal amount. You can then back into the full funding goal with that number.

For example, if you have 100 people you can reasonably expect to contribute to your campaign, and you estimate that the average pledge or funding amount from each is $50, you would calculate your funding amount as follows:

100 x $50 = $5000

$5000 = 40% of your funding goal.

To solve for your funding goal:

$5000 divided by .40 (40%) = $12,500

Now you try:

_____ (core number of people)

x

_____ (avg. donation expected) = _____ / .40

= _____ (your funding goal!)

Help! What to do when there's a difference between what your funding calculation indicates, what you can reasonably raise, and what you need to get your project off the ground.

It's possible that you may need more money than you can reasonably expect to raise in order to complete your project. If this is the case, think about breaking your project down into phases such as "pre-production," "production," and "post- production." This is what I did with my conference. The total amount I needed to raise was $45,000 but I knew my community would unlikely produce that amount of funding. I segmented my project into three separate campaigns based on the staging of the event. My initial campaign created so much additional support in the form of sponsor dollars and follow up contributions that the two additional campaigns to cover production and post-production costs were unnecessary.

Another option you have is to critically evaluate your project. You may see it as one big project, but is it possible that there are two or three projects within your one big project? If so, you can do multiple campaigns over a period of time for these individual sub- projects.

Breaking your project down into small sub-projects can be challenging for some people.

If you'd like help working on this with a certified expert, check out my Additional Services page at **pattylennon.com/services**

Money Mindset

It's possible, that as you look at these numbers and consider asking for contributions, that you are feeling nervous, upset, scared, or overwhelmed. It's ok. Money brings up people's stuff. In western society there is an intense connection between money and self-worth, confidence, sense of security and so much more.

Anything that has the whiff of "asking for money" or "needing money" is uncomfortable for most people.

Fears create money mindset issues. These issues show up in a number of ways. Maybe you struggle with having sales conversations in your business. Perhaps your bank account does not look like what you want it to look like. Maybe the thought of asking for help leaves you queasy.

If you are experiencing any of this it may make sense to get some support around shifting your money mindset. There are a number of qualified coaches that do this work.

I regularly work with people in my private coaching practice on their money mindsets.

If you'd like to discuss working together on this issue I'd love to speak with you!
You can email me at **Patty@PattyLennon.com**

Cleaning up our money issues is beneficial for us, and for the generations to come!

CHAPTER FIVE:
THE POWER OF YOUR INNER CIRCLE

Harnessing the power of your inner circle is critical to the success of your campaign. Most likely, when you considered the people you could reasonably rely on to contribute to your campaign you were thinking about your inner circle. That is because this is your first line of defense in funding.

Your inner circle is the people who will support you if you show them how to do it. Your inner circle typically consists of friends and family. Often times, asking for help from those nearest and dearest to us is uncomfortable. In this chapter, we're going to:

- Uncover your inner circle.

- Create a communication plan to get the word out to this valuable group of people.

- Address the mindset issues that can derail your success when asking for support

Sometimes we lose track of how many people we know and who would be there for us if we showed them we needed help. Let's create a list of your inner circle so that confusion doesn't happen!

Right now, do a "brain dump" of everyone you know. For this exercise, I prefer using an excel spreadsheet to compile contacts. I suggest keeping it simple. Populate it with the following information:

- First Name

- Last Name

- Company

- Category (I'll explain this later on)

When I started doing this for my campaign, I made this much more complicated than it needed to be. I had lots and lots of columns. By the end of my campaign, I had hidden every column but these four, which is why I suggest you keep it simple.

If you have an electronic address book or some other contact management system, you can export that to an excel file to begin. To save time, do this before you start adding to the list. Keep in mind that just because someone is in your address book doesn't necessarily mean they are part of your inner circle. This is where the category column on your list is most helpful. There, you can make a note of whether the person is part of your inner circle or not.

Next, scan your social media accounts to see if you've missed anyone that you consider your "inner circle."

Finally, spend five to ten minutes a few days a week adding to the list. Perhaps you'll run into someone you haven't seen in a while, and they can be added to the list, or as you review your list, one name will trigger another. Continue to do this everyday until you can think of no one else to add to the list—then do it for another week.

Once your list is complete, review the entire thing and categorize the people on this list. The category titles you assign aren't important just yet. You should be able glance at the list and find the people you need when you need them, especially those in your inner circle.

For instance, you may use categories such as

- Inner circle

- Colleague

- Blogger

- Media contact

Leave the category blank if you are unsure how to categorize a person. You may not know them well. You'll still want to reach out to them at some point and alert them about your campaign but you won't include them in your inner circle.

Give a special category to the people who have committed to contributing to your campaign. These people in particular are very important because you will want to solicit commitments for contributions totaling approximately $1000 to be made on day one of your campaign.

These day-one contributors help your campaign increase its perceived viability by bulking up your funding at the start of your campaign. When potential contributors visit the campaign and see that there are already contributions totaling $1000 on day one, the campaign *feels* like it will succeed. Conveying the viability of your project in every way possible is critical to transforming potential contributors into actual contributors.

Engage

Your inner circle wants to help you! It is unlikely that everyone you know will be able to support you with money, but all can support you by spreading the word. In order to help them help you, you must engage your inner circle in a way that connects to their hearts and their heads.

In your communication to your inner circle, you will want to be vulnerable and use the words "I need help." This is very challenging for most people. Our society encourages pride in *doing it on your own*. Being vulnerable is scary. However, I can tell you from personal experience that using the words "I need help" has a powerful and positive effect on everything you do; crowdfunding is no exception.

I want you to be prepared to ask for help confidently when the time comes, so over the next four weeks I have a mindset-shifting exercise that will get your help-asking muscles in shape! Asking for help gets easier the more you practice, so over the next four weeks complete the following:

In **week one**, ask for help at least once a day, and receive it openly with a gracious thank you.

In **week two**, ask for help at least twice a day, and receive it openly each time with a gracious thank you.

In **week three**, ask for help at least three times a day, and receive it openly each time with a gracious thank you.

In **week four**, ask for help at least four times a day, and receive it openly each time with a gracious thank you.

To cultivate even more benefit from this exercise, journal about your experience as you move through it. I've included a sample journal page to get you started.

Help Me Please! Exercise

JOURNAL EACH DAY AND INCLUDE ANSWERS TO
THE FOLLOWING:

Day:_____

Request Made: _____

_____

_____

_____

_____

Results: _____

_____

_____

_____

_____

How I felt: _____

_____

_____

_____

_____

If you are a giver by nature, this four-week exercise may be particularly challenging. I want to offer you some understanding about the value you **give** to the world when you ask and accept help. We are inter-relational beings. We are meant to live and work in relationship to others. In order for that to happen, giving and receiving must occur in balance. What would happen if people only gave and never received?

I think we can all agree, as we look around, that the world is a little out of balance. There are entire countries struggling to feed their children. There are places where war, destruction, and violence are a part of every day life. The key to shifting this paradigm is within each and every one of us. When we create more balance in our own existence it has a ripple effect.

If you are giving much more than you are receiving that is creating an imbalance in **your** world and that has a ripple effect, as well. For the sake of more balance in the world, please learn to ask *and* accept help!

Learning to ask for help and being able to accept it graciously is a gift. As you expand that gift you will notice that not only will your crowdfunding campaign benefit from your new, and strong "help-asking muscles," you will start to notice dramatic shifts in your life as well!

Communication Plan

Now that you are a help-asking, graciously-accepting support machine, let's put a communication plan together to harness the power of your nearest and dearest friends!

One week before your campaign starts, send out an email (or letter) to your inner circle alerting them to the campaign. Depending on the length of the campaign, email them once or twice about the success you are having, and remind them that you still need help.

Note: Your inner circle list is not the same as the list of people you have met along the way who have specifically said they will support the campaign. It is possible that some of your inner circle will be on that list as well, and you can choose which communication these people should receive. In the case of your inner circle communication, you should speak to them in a voice that communicates that they are your nearest and dearest.

In all your communications be sure to include the call to action that will remind your potential contributors how they can help you. This call to action will highlight three possible opportunities:

- Contribute to the campaign.

- Spread the word.

- Leave a comment.

The day your campaign starts send out an email (or letter) to your inner circle alerting them to the fact that the campaign has gone live. This email will be much shorter than the previous email. I recommend structuring it as follows:

- Remind your inner circle about the email you already sent.

- Remind them you need help.

- Share your call to action.

Throughout the campaign email updates to your inner circle. If something significant happens or you reach a major milestone let them know that. You can simply thank many of them who have already supported the campaign and give a progress report on where you are with the campaign.

Always end your correspondence with your call to action to contribute, spread the word, and leave a comment on your campaign page.

I encourage you to write at least these first two emails before the campaign launches. This will soften the workload you have around the time of your campaign. If you find you are struggling with writing emails, know that you are not alone.

Creating written communications can be challenging for some people. This may be a good place in your campaign to engage support. If you have a friend or family member who is particularly gifted at writing, ask them for help. One of the places I create ease in my Crowdfund With Ease™ program is by supplying templates for all these communications to all participants.

If you feel this would be beneficial to you, find registration information for the program here: pattylennon.com/CFWE

Prewritten Correspondence

In your call to action you ask your inner circle to "spread the word." Getting your people to tell their people about your campaign will help the campaign grow and its funding increase. One of the simplest ways to increase the number of people spreading the word for you is to make it easy on them.

You do this by providing pre-written communication that is ready to send. This means emails they can cut, paste, and send. It also means social media posts such as those for Twitter and Facebook.

Generally, you can use the emails you've written to send to your own audience and restructure them to make sense for your inner circle. You do this by changing references of "I" and "me" . For example, if in your email template you write:

Dear Friends and Family,

I need your help.

You could change it to read:

Dear Friends and Family,

My cousin/friend/sister, Patty, needs your help.

Voila, you have a pre-written email for you cousin, sister, or best friend to send on your behalf.

A sample Facebook posts would look like this:

I have a dear friend who is creating a big change for [insert name of group that will benefit from your campaign]. Please visit here [insert link to campaign] and leave a comment cheering her on.

A sample Twitter post would look like this:

[Insert campaign name] will be a groundbreaking event. Join the movement! [insert short link]

We'll dive a bit deeper into social media in Chapter Seven, but if writing social media is not your strength there are a number of social media consultants and copywriters that can help you with this. I also provide social media templates in my course, Crowdfund with Ease™.

The Crowdfund with Ease™ Program is available at **pattylennon.com/CFWE**

Recognize

As people support you by funding your campaign and sharing your campaign link, be sure to thank them and recognize their contributions.

A wonderful way to engage a part of your inner circle at a deeper level is to recognize the contribution they make to your life, and in this case, to your crowdfunding campaign. A few ways to do this are to:

- Make your advocates your ambassadors.

- Record video testimonials.

- Mention them in public and on social media.

Ambassadors

Depending on your crowdfunding platform, you may be able to list your team members individually on the campaign page. Having "ambassadors" as part of your team can be a win-win. The more people you have on your team, the greater the perceived viability of your project.

An ambassador is simply someone who plays an active role in getting the world out about your campaign throughout the campaign's duration. Listing ambassadors gives you a way to recognize people who are advocating for your campaign.

You'll want to be careful who you choose, and limit ambassadors to the three to five people who are willing and able to be out there on the front lines, shouting about your campaign from the rooftops. Ideally, these people have large and strong social connections.

Brainstorm a list of potential ambassadors here:

1. _____

2. _____

3. _____

4. _____

5. _____

6. _____

7. _____

8. _____

9. _____

10. _____

A printable version of this worksheet is
available at **pattylennon.com/worksheets**

Once you have chosen your ambassadors, a great way to keep them interested and excited about your campaign is to run contests between them. You can give out small gifts for the ambassador who generates the most contributions to the campaign each week. You can create a bonus for any ambassador that brings in a milestone contribution such as the contribution that takes you over the 50% mark. What you do with a contest is really only limited by your creativity. The key is to keep your ambassadors focused on getting the word out and driving traffic to your crowdfunding site.

After the release of the first edition of this book many questions arose about building an Ambassador Team, especially as people launched campaigns and were disappointed in the support they received from their ambassadors. There were some consistent mistakes I found most people made that were disappointed in their ambassador teams. Here are the big mistakes I found most people were making and how to avoid making those same mistakes in your own campaign.

Mistake #1 Too Many Ambassadors.

Its important to keep your ambassador team small. Three to five ambassadors is the ideal size of your team. This is truly a place where quality over quantity wins. If you don't have experience leading or managing teams stick to 2–3 team members.

Mistake #2 Choosing Ambassadors Lacking Key Skills

Choose your team members based on their skill sets. You want team members that are enthusiastic about your campaign but enthusiasm without action will not get the job done. Ideal ambassadors have one or more of the following strengths:

- Networking

- Fundraising

- Social Networking

- Social Media

- Communication

- Boldness

An ambassador does not need to encompass all of these skill sets but they should have at least one. And all ambassadors need to have one unique trait—the ability to take action! Which leads me to the final mistake many people who experienced disappointment with their ambassador team made.

Mistake #3 Ignoring Who People Truly Are

Maya Angelou once said "When people show you who they are, believe them." This is valuable advice when forming your ambassador team. As I consulted with various people in the midst of their campaign that were struggling with inactive ambassadors, it became clear that the warning signs were available long before the campaign started.

When we examined how an ambassador had shown up in her life prior to being invited onto the ambassador team they had a history of being "big talkers" that rarely took action on all that talk. These people are often fun to have around. Their enthusiasm is contagious but they rarely DO anything with that enthusiasm.

These "big talkers" always had an excuse on why they weren't able to follow through.

Because these people are so fun to have around there is nothing wrong with engaging that enthusiasm throughout the campaign, just don't make them a part of the ambassador team you need taking action to get the word out.

When you avoid these three big mistakes when building your ambassador team you'll power up your potential for success!

Once you have your team in place its important to keep them motivated. Keeping a team engaged is a skill and if you don't have experience with team building you may lose sight of what is important.

In order to keep your team inspired and active, focus on these five key leadership traits.

#1 Set Clear Goals

When bringing an ambassador on your team, explain the goals you have for your ambassador and how those goals fit into the larger goals of your crowdfunding campaign.

Also get clear on what your ambassador's goals are. Understand why they are participating as an ambassador on your team. For most ambassadors the answer will simply be that they love you and what you do and want to help you succeed. However, on occasion a person may be willing to help you in exchange for you helping them further down the road. It's important to understand that motivation before you work together.

#2 Communicate Consistently

You must stay in touch with your ambassadors regularly. How you communicate with them is less important with the fact that it happens repeatedly. A weekly check in, along with updates on key occurrences like milestones or press mentions is important to keeping your ambassador team engaged and connected to your campaign. Here are a few ways you can organize your communication:

- Email

- Private Facebook group

- Host conference calls

- Weekly In Person meetings (if everyone is local)

- Skype Calls

#3 Make It Fun

Host contests for your ambassadors and announce the winner at your weekly check in. You can have the same contest each week or change it up weekly. The primary job of the ambassador is to bring people to your campaign (and ideally people who contribute) so its important to build the contests around those activities. Here are some contest ideas to get you started:

Most referrals made through social media

- Biggest donation

- Milestone contributor

- Largest number of donations

- Most active social media post

Contest prizes don't need to be expensive, they need to be fun! Think about what your people love and build prizes around that. (Note: If you are raising large dollars where you are relying on ambassadors to bring in big contributors it makes sense to have at least one contest prize that reflects that value.)

#4 Show Appreciation

Your ambassadors agreed to support you because they want to be of service to you. The contests will keep it fun but the true reward for your ambassadors is knowing they helped you. Showing your appreciation is the greatest gift you can give this amazing group of supportive team members.

Say thank you often and let your ambassadors feel the love! Saying "thank you" sounds obvious but during the fast pace of your campaign you may lose track of this simple act. You can do this by text, email or social media. If you really want to pump up the appreciation do something that involves a bit more personal connection. Here are a few quick and easy ways to thank your team members that will have a big impact:

- Replace a text with a live call

- Snail Mail a thank you

- Send a $5 coffee card if they've been up late getting the word out about your campaign

- Post a 15 seconds thank you video to their Facebook page

- Brag about their awesomeness to their family members in front of them

During your campaign your time will be limited but showing your appreciation for an active ambassador is worth the extra effort!

#5 Celebrate Success!
If you focus on setting clear goals, consistent communication, keeping it fun and showing appreciation you'll have an ambassador team that will carry you to the finish line on their shoulders! When you get to the finish line pop open a bottle of champagne (or a box of chocolates) and celebrate your collective success!

Let your team experience their contribution to your success and you'll turn your crowdfunding ambassadors into a long term advocates!

Video Testimonials

Including video testimonials of some of your nearest and dearest in your pitch video is another way to recognize those closest to the campaign. This also gives them a way to promote your campaign to their circle by sending out email and social media posts that say things like:

> *Check out my testimonial for [your name or project name] at [your campaign link]. I just love what she is doing!*

Even if you can't include these testimonials in your pitch video, you can record them and add them to either the media section of your campaign, or you can send them out as an update. This still allows for the person giving the testimonial to draw the attention of his inner circle to your campaign.

Not everyone enjoys being on film so this is a good opportunity only if the person *likes* to do video. I love doing video, so will always hop in front of a camera for my nearest and dearest! Some of my friends would rather have root canals than have to speak on camera, so make sure you target wisely!

Note: If you are going to include someone on a video testimonial in your pitch video, be sure to give them the questions you'd like them to answer on camera ahead of time. Request that they give you their answers in writing prior to filming, so you can guide them to the answers that best showcase your campaign. Brainstorm some potential video testimonials here:

1. _____

2. _____

3. _____

4. _____

5. _____

6. _____

7. _____

8. _____

9. _____

10. _____

(Note: You can refer back to Chapter 3 for tips on how to film a great testimonial.)

Public Mentions

The best way to keep the support flowing through your campaign is to give people public kudos when they support you. You can do this any number of ways, but here are some suggestions:

• Tag supporters on Facebook and Twitter.

• Reply to comments on your crowdfunding platform.

- Mention contributors at social gatherings.

- Mention them in follow-up emails to your inner circle.

- Tell other people about their kindness (I always find this makes its way back to people).

- If a family member contributes, call up their mother, daughter, or sister and mention how much their support meant to you.

This isn't just to keep the momentum going on your campaign. There are emotional and spiritual benefits to focusing on publicly recognizing support. Many people feel invisible today. Helping someone feel "seen" is important work.

Our media outlets primarily focus on what is wrong with society. Shouting out the good people in your life reminds those who are listening that there is more good in the world than bad; that alone creates some powerful and positive karma for all of us!

CHAPTER SIX
YOUR ONLINE CAMPAIGN

In this chapter, I'll walk you through the key aspects of setting up your campaign:

1. Video Pitch

2. Your Funding Goal

3. Project Headline

4. Project Summary

5. Rewards

1. Video Pitch

You completed the work you need to do for your video pitch in Chapter Three, so you are already ahead of the game! Congratulations!

2. Your Funding Goal

In Chapter Four you calculated how much you could reasonably expect to fund. This equation is not based in science, so just use it as a guideline. Also, look to your intuitive voice or "gut" for guidance when setting your funding amount.

Remember, every individual's ability to fundraise is different. If you believe you can raise more than this calculation indicates, go for it! In relation to your marketing plan, just keep in mind that your funding amount can encourage or discourage people from donating. If you set it too high and it just doesn't seem reachable, people will be less likely to donate.

If you set it too low, you may reach your funding goal early—which is great—but there will be a portion of your contributors who may not donate once you've reached your goal; their motivation is strictly to see you succeed, and not necessarily for the reward they will receive by contributing to the campaign.

Choose a stretch amount that will challenge your fundraising efforts, but choose an amount that is realistic for your circumstances.

3. Project Headline

With new platforms popping up each day, it's hard to capture what each platform calls this title of your campaign. Most refer to it as either your tagline or your headline. Either way it is highly visible. Here is an example:

Here is an example of your project headline in your widget:

Be creative when choosing your headline! A great tagline or headline grabs people's attention and makes them want to find out more. This doesn't have to be complicated.

Here are some examples of good headlines:

Let's Build A Goddamn Tesla Museum
pattylennon.com/tesla

This headline grabbed my attention the minute I saw it. The "Let's" immediately makes the reader feel part of the mission. When I was first researching crowdfunding this project was my favorite because Matthew Inman's passion for his project came through in everything he did related to the campaign, starting with the headline.

Kreyos: The ONLY Smartwatch With Voice & Gesture Control
pattylennon.com/kreyos

Although I don't care that much about smartwatches, if I were an early adopter (which is their target funder) this would make me read more. Capitalizing the "ONLY" draws attention to what is unique about the product.

Newlywed and Broke: A New Single-Camera Comedy
pattylennon.com/newlywed-and-broke

The title made me smile and anything that makes me smile grabs my attention.

Touching Strangers: Photographs by Richard Renaldi
pattylennon.com/richard-renaldi

What drew me in here was the idea that someone might have gone around touching strangers which in our society is a bit off center. I wasn't sure how that could play out. By simply piquing my curiosity, the campaigner caused me to click through.

Drawstring Backpack Reinvented
pattylennon.com/backpack

My son loves drawstring backpacks so the fact that they were recreating something I am closely familiar with made me stop and look.

As you scan the front pages of crowdfunding sites, watch what headlines call to you and make you click through to read/watch/hear more. This will give you an idea of what works for your people. Remember, you are the best indicator of what **your** people will like.

There is no right way to do this. Make it fun. Grab a few friends that understand what you're doing, head down to your favorite watering hole, and buy a couple of rounds of drinks. You'll have a great headline in no time. Once you have chosen your kick butt headline, write it down.

My Kick Butt Headline is: _____

_____

4. Project Summary

Your project summary is the body of the main page of your crowdfunding campaign.

STRUCTURING YOUR PROJECT SUMMARY

- Put the most important information at the top, least important at the bottom.

- Make it easy to read, clear, and concise; the fewer words the better.

- Use headings, subheadings, bolded words, and pictures so your summary is visually easy for readers to follow.

- Use media to make it pop. (Logos, picture of product, team members, or rewards are all great options).

CREATING YOUR PROJECT SUMMARY

1. Restate your *Big Why*_____

_____

_____

2. What is different about your product, service or project?

_____

_____

_____

3. Who needs your project, service or project?

_____

_____

_____

4. Describe the viability of this venture. Why are you going to succeed?_____

_____

_____

5. Provide your background and your team's background if it ties to your campaign or supports its viability.

_____

_____

_____

6. What will you use your funding for? Include a budget if possible._____

_____

_____

When it comes to marketing, project summaries are the backup plan. Your pitch video and rewards should do the heavy lifting where your marketing is concerned. So don't stress too much about this section.

Looking back, I spent an unnecessary amount of time trying to make this section perfect. The reality is, most of your contributors won't even read this section unless you are relying on high dollar contributions.

5. Creating Rewards

I really struggled when crafting my rewards. I ping-ponged between coming up with creative names for rewards and then backing into what might be included in a reward with that name. Please learn from my mistakes! Naming your rewards is an important part of the process, but figuring out what your rewards are is more important. Rewards first, names second.

When I work with clients privately reward creation is one of the areas where we spend a significant amount of time so I created a system to simplify the process, which I'll share with you now.

PATTY'S SUPER DUPER 3D REWARD CREATION SYSTEM:

- **D**ollar Amount

- **D**istribution

- **D**escription

DOLLAR AMOUNT

I recommend using the following standard reward amounts:

- $5 or $10

- $25 (this is the most popular contribution amount)

- $50

- $100

- $250

(Higher dollar rewards should also be "standard amounts," like $500, $1000, and $2000.)

Unless you have a really good reason for using other types of denominations (like $3, $33, $133), please don't get creative with dollar amounts. Remember, most people are going to visit your site to support you or your mission. The reward is an added bonus. Pick the amounts *you* are used to seeing when you look to contribute to an effort or project.

If you're considering offering a $1 reward, choose $5 over $1. People will contribute $5 just as easily as $1, and you'll receive far more money if the first reward listed is $5 rather than $1.

If you are funding product creation or manufacturing don't use retail pricing such as $149 to set your reward amount simply because this is how much that reward would go for at your online store. A common mistake I see people make when they are funding product manufacturing is incorporating retail pricing into their reward amount, which makes your crowdfunding page look like a sales page or shopping cart. If you want to mention that a reward offers a discount off retail pricing, that's smart, but pricing the way you would price for retail is just plain confusing to your contributors.

The argument I've heard from clients is that they need to offer their widget at $27 in order to clear their costs. They can't possibly offer it at $25 (a standard crowdfunding reward amount.) I completely understand and I don't want you to lose money. I also don't want to see you confuse your contributors. So if you are struggling with a similar situation figure out what you can *add* to your widget to get it up to $50 or remove from your widget to get it down to $25.

Choose your dollar amounts **then** design rewards with these dollar amounts in mind.

Great rewards:

- Directly tie to you or the campaign

- Don't require independent sales efforts

- Have obvious benefits (inside scoop, early delivery, intimate setting)

Ideas for Rewards
Low Dollar ($5, $10):

- A reminder that the contributor is making something happen with their donation (e.g. "With this donation, you'll sleep well knowing you are helping to send books to children in impoverished countries.")

- A heart-felt thank you (i.e. "From the bottom of my heart I thank you. You are making a difference in my world and the world of many, many children.")

- Exclusive access to an electronic download (video, music, e-book).

- Name listed on website as supporter

Middle Dollar ($25 — $250):

These benefits generally tie directly to what you're funding.

- Early distribution of product.

- Service bundles.

- Event tickets.

High Dollar ($250+):

- Intimate gatherings.

- Special access to you or your project.

- A special role in your project or business (producer credits, taste tester, naming a product)

Sponsor Reward

If you are looking to attract sponsors for your project, offering a high dollar reward designed to benefit those sponsors can be a great marketing technique. Don't expect a sponsor just to find you and contribute to your campaign because of this reward, but if you are already in communication with a potential sponsor, alerting them to this increased visibility opportunity is a great option.

The best place to find ideas for your rewards is from other campaigns. Check back on the campaigns that interested you and see how they designed their rewards. Look at the campaigns that are on the front page of Indiegogo and Kickstarter, which generally feature high performing campaigns. If a campaign is doing well, it likely has some great rewards!

As you design your rewards be sure you are able to deliver what you are offering in a timely way. This brings us to the second D of Patty's Super Duper 3D Reward Creation System.

Distribution

T-shirts with your logo or project's picture on it may seem like a great reward, but they are a pain in the backside to manage from the perspective of distribution. Do you really want to be sitting in your living room, individually packing and shipping fifty t-shirts to donors? I can answer that for you—no, you don't!

If you have a distribution team or distribution system built into your business, this may not be an issue. But if you are like most of us and the distribution team is just *you*, then please factor in the effort and cost involved in distributing each reward. You may still offer that reward, but do it at a higher dollar level where the effort involved makes sense.

Also, be sure to factor in the amount of time it will take you to reasonably distribute your rewards, *then double it* before you set your delivery date. For example, if you think it will take you three months after your campaign ends to get your product out, tell your contributors they can expect to see it in six months.

There is a certain amount of optimism that surges through a person's veins as he contemplates finally receiving the money needed to move a project forward. **Do not** allow optimism to dictate your targeted delivery dates for your rewards. Remember the key to happy customers (or in this case, contributors): **under-promise, over-deliver**.

Once you have your rewards designed and the dollar amounts assigned to each, write them here: (you can leave the name blank for now; we'll cover that next):

Reward #1

$_____

Name: _____

Brief description: _____

_____

Reward #1

$_____

Name: _____

Brief description: _____

_____

Reward #1

$_____

Name: _____

Brief description: _____

_____

Reward #1

$_____

Name: _____

Brief description: _____

_____

Description

Okay! We are up to the third D of Patty's Super Duper 3D Reward Creation System. Now we can get down to naming these rewards. Find a theme that ties to your campaign and build a series of reward names that relate to that theme. Again, don't over think this. Have fun!

Get those friends that helped you with your headline back together. Bribe them with a few more rounds of drinks and work on your reward names together. Having a few people to bounce ideas around with is very helpful at this stage. Once you are done, fill in the names of your rewards above.

Bonus Rewards

Bonus rewards are limited-opportunity, limited-number rewards that pop up throughout your campaign for a short period of time. Think of them as a flash sale for your crowd-funding campaign.

A bonus reward can be anything that your potential contributors would enjoy receiving or experiencing. The purpose of the bonus reward is twofold; one to create a reason to send out fresh communications; and, two, to create excitement and interest around your campaign.

As an example, some of the bonus rewards I offered were:

- A free hotel stay the night before my conference

- Spa gift basket

- Massage

- Expensive chocolates

In each case, there was only one reward available. Each was partnered with a ticket to the Mom Gets a Business [*] Conference.

Note: Bonus rewards are a great way to harness the power of business partners that want to support you. Each of the bonus rewards I offered were donated by local businesses, so although the dollar amount of the reward offered was much more than the reward for a conference ticket alone, there were no out-of-pocket costs to our campaign. In exchange for these products, I talked about these reward sponsors in social media and other communications. Win-win!

Do you have any partners or potential sponsors that could benefit from the added exposure that your campaign could bring them? Approach them to donate a reward or two to add to your bonus rewards!

The timing of when to release bonus rewards does not need to be decided before you launch. You'll want to keep your bonus rewards in your "back pocket" and push them live when you see that activity on your campaign is slowing down.

CHAPTER SEVEN
YOUR MARKETING PLAN

When I first launched my business I thought I understood how to market. I had held a number of senior positions in my banking career, half of which involved sales. I created marketing material and regularly participated in planning and executing marketing launches.

I expected that all this work history would naturally prepare me to be a successful marketer when I was on my own. What I didn't understand was how much work the marketing department did for me back in my corporate life. They created structure to our marketing launches and guidelines for the creation of marketing materials. This, paired with the direction from our leadership team, created the Marketing Plan.

Once I was out on my own, without structure or guidelines, very little of what I did seemed to have any effect—positive or negative—on my business. My marketing consisted of throwing anything I could think of up against the wall and watching to see what would stick. But even when something did stick I didn't do anything with that information. I didn't create more opportunity for myself based on what was working.

I was so overwhelmed with everything I had to do that I was constantly reactive, and not active. Luckily I figured this out and hired someone to teach me how to shift my perspective. I learned how to set a course for my business, to create a marketing plan, and follow it. And that is when my business started growing. You need the same skill set to be a successful crowdfunder.

As I mentioned in Chapter Three, being able to promote yourself—to *market* yourself—is the key to succeeding at crowdfunding. Creating a plan is the only way to market successfully without getting overwhelmed or lost in the process. The five key aspects of your marketing plan are:

1. Social Media

2. Campaign Updates

3. Email Correspondence

4. Blogs

5. Your Website

Social Media

Crowdfunding relies heavily on social media to spread the word about your campaign. The social media channels available to you are endless so, as I mentioned in Chapter Two, focus on the one or two sites where your potential contributors spend the most time. In this chapter you'll learn how to harness the power of some of the most commonly used social media options—Twitter, Facebook, LinkedIn, Instagram, and Pinterest.

It's important to update social media regularly. Becoming active on a new social media site just because you are launching a campaign will probably not provide you the traction you need. Plan to spend three to six months on a social media platform prior to launch to build up a following. Social media is about being "social" and you can't create real relationships in a few days.

I asked some of the social media experts I know to give you help in using some of the most popular social media platforms to promote your campaign.

Simple Strategies to Capture Attention for Your Crowdfunding Campaign on Facebook and Twitter

CRYSTAL GIRGENTI

In today's digital world, social media has brought us closer as a community and has expanded our reach, allowing us to connect with businesses and a growing number of individuals, like never before. We now have the chance to easily share information with the masses and gather feedback about our products and services before we even launch them. With this opportunity, using social media has become crucial in achieving a successful crowdfunding campaign.

When running a crowdfunding campaign, there is no magic

bullet. It requires a lot of hard work before, during, and after your campaign. The number one reason crowdfunding campaigns fail to get funded is because the crowdfunder's network wasn't properly prepared. You want a network of individuals who are pumped, primed, and ready to support you and your idea.

A Facebook audience has consistently been the number one source of backing for most crowdfunders, with Twitter not far behind. Based on research done on crowdfunding, we know that approximately 30—40% of your funding (sometimes much more) will come from your personal network—if it's built properly. You want to make sure that you set up these accounts and start building your audience in advance, so that when you launch your campaign, your network is ready to give.

For crowdfunders looking to fund their dreams, this can be where they become overwhelmed, and the lack of knowledge of how to use social media can become a distraction. With a basic understanding and the implementation of a few promotional strategies, you will maximize your chances of success and will be well on your way to building a business around your passion.

Social media is all about building relationships, so it's essential to allow the necessary time to connect with others and establish relationships before your campaign. Allow yourself at least 60—90 days before launching your campaign to build your audience. Building relationships is not all about just connecting with everyone and promoting your campaign. You want to connect with other people authentically and organically and start engaging in conversations. By being authentic and acting with integrity, you will build more loyal relationships with people who'll stay connected and support you for the long haul.

While there are many pieces and strategies to consider when promoting your crowdfunding campaign, you don't have to spend a lot of money. You do, however, have to invest your time. But with a successful, fully funded campaign, it will all be worth the effort. Here are a few ways to use Facebook and Twitter (for free) to gain the attention of the backers you need.

Facebook

Your personal friend network on Facebook, prior to launching your campaign, can be the main factor in determining your odds of success. Set a goal to have at least 100 personal friends, ones that you know or have something in common with. If we look only at the number of friends as a predictive factor, we find that the more friends, the greater your chances of getting funded.

However, it's not only the sheer number of friends that will fund your dream. It's the positive relationships you build. The 60–90 day timeframe prior to your launch is a critical phase in your campaign. Use this time to engage in conversations with other friends. You'll want to comment on their posts with uplifting and supportive responses, add value to their lives with inspiring quotes or helpful recommendations, or share a heartwarming story. People always remember how you made them feel. With positive feelings towards you, your friends will be more willing to support you when it's your launch time. This is the "Likeability Campaign" Patty refers to earlier in the book.

Before launching, sit down and start building a list of benefits for your product or business. This is really going to help you get focused on the results for donors and buyers and less on the promotion. No one likes to be sold to and that goes for crowdfunding too.

During your campaign, aim to post every day using both your personal profile and your business page. Inform your audience about the good that comes from your idea, how it will help others, and what's in it for them, so they can know where they're putting their money. If you're using your campaign to pre-sell your product, let your audience know about the exclusive offers for backers.

Be prepared to tell your story. Why is this idea so important to you? Is it a passion of yours? Do you have a family story? How did you think of it? This will help people connect with you on a higher level— rather than just simply reading a crowdfunding campaign website. When people can connect with you and feel that they know, like, and trust you, they're more willing to support you during and after your campaign.

On your Facebook business page, your posts are only seen by a small number of fans. This number has declined over the past couple of years and may continue to do so as Facebook introduces paid options for showing posts. With this in mind, if you are not seeing the traffic that you thought you would, reach out to your close contacts or ones you think may be willing to back you by private message. It is very likely that friends, colleagues, or business connections simply didn't see your posts. Briefly tell them your story and a little about your campaign. Politely remind them about the deadline and ask them to consider donating. This may take a great deal of your time, but you should see an increase in your backers and funding immediately.

Another effortless strategy is to offer stretch goals based upon Facebook shares or fans. Stretch goals offer additional rewards for backers when a certain target is reached. For example, if you were crowdfunding for the capital to publish a book, you could add an additional format or another chapter if you reach 200 shares of your Facebook page with the campaign listed. As an alternative, you could specify that with the addition of a predetermined number of fans on your page, you will reduce the amount needed to reach a stretch goal. Be sure to update your backers and your audience on the progress of these marks.

The assumption with these stretch goals is: that with more followers or shares, you'll receive additional backers. You must always be cautious that your stretch goals do not leave your project over budget or behind schedule, thus negatively impacting your campaign.

Just because your campaign has ended, don't think your job

is over. Use your Facebook page to update your audience on the progress of development, manufacturing, or partnerships. And most importantly, show your appreciation to your backers by thanking them and keeping them in the loop.

Twitter

The stretch goal strategy can also be applied to Twitter followers or retweets. Like Facebook, you should use Twitter to build relationships and drive traffic to your campaign.

Start building an audience by following industry leaders and sharing valuable and helpful content. With Twitter, you'll want to create and post at least 3—4 times per day. These posts can be original or can help your audience spread a message by retweeting their content. It's important to make these messages different so you look authentic and human. Don't forget to post updates, new rewards, and progress reports to your backers, and offer thanks and appreciation mentioning your followers in the tweet. In addition, be sure to tweet a link to any blog or media mentions you receive.

Tracking the effectiveness of a tweet can be difficult, but with the proper tools, you'll gain valuable insight as to what's working and what you need to adjust. Using a URL-shortener, such as bit.ly or goo.gl, can track clicks, giving you helpful stats about your efforts. Create these links for your crowdfunding campaign page and include them in every tweet.

Another way to get traffic and awareness is to utilize hashtags. Within Twitter, hashtags are the "#" symbol followed by a relevant word that allows anyone to search for a common interest. You can create your own hashtag and allow people to follow you. At the very least, you can use the hashtag "#crowdfunding" in each tweet to take full advantage of this feature.

As with most social media sites, the secret to maximizing exposure is to reach the fans and followers of your audience. An easy way to do this is to just ask your audience to share or retweet. By including a polite "Pls RT" (i.e. please retweet) before your link, you'll see an increase in followers and backers. Follow up by mentioning the person who shared your message, saying "thanks for sharing" and you'll soon gain a loyal following that knows you are worth their effort and money.

The crowdfunding community is built of people looking to help others. Use your social media sites to connect with others who have crowdfunded an idea, fully funded or not, and create conversations. You can learn from these individuals and gain their support. With the implementation of these strategies and a "never give up" positive attitude, you'll be on your way to funding success!

Linking to Contributors with LinkedIn

SALVADOR BRIGGMAN

LinkedIn is a great resource for connecting with influencers and potential backers. Still, a lot of people don't have a profile or don't understand how it can factor into their social media promotion strategy. Whether through interest-centric groups, surveys, InMails, introductions, or lead generation, LinkedIn is an invaluable tool for crowdfunding and business success. I've included a few tips below to demonstrate how you can use LinkedIn to garner support for your idea, project, or business.

Before executing on any of these tips, ensure that your LinkedIn profile has a current professional photograph, a descriptive work history (including skills and education), and that you have a made a few connections with your Gmail, Yahoo!, or Hotmail accounts, or by using the "people you may know" tool.

The above steps serve to confirm your identity and legitimacy, and they make it more likely that people will respond to your messages or engage in a discussion you create. Requesting LinkedIn recommendations are also a great way to show the world that you have a strong worth ethic and have successfully worked with people in the past. Here are four tips for promoting your crowdfunding campaign.

1. LinkedIn Advanced Search

By using LinkedIn Advanced search, you can find influencers or potential backers via keywords, location, industry, interests, and seniority level. To access some of the more valuable search items, like the groups a person is involved in, or their years of experience, you may need to purchase a premium account. Either way, this capability is powerful for lead generation.

For example, if you were running an education-based crowdfunding campaign and wanted to connect with bloggers, entrepreneurs, teachers, or professionals in this industry, you could use advanced search to concentrate on individuals in your area, working at a particular education nonprofit, who in the past went to your alma mater. The individuals who appear in these search results are potential leads.

They may be willing to connect you with the education nonprofit for a partnership, forward the campaign to their friends in the education industry, or be willing to support it themselves because you are from their alma mater. You can also use the first, second, and third degree connection tool to identify professionals who are connected to you in some way.

For example, let's say you have a design industry Kickstarter product. If you were looking to connect with people who blog about design, by using advanced search you could see if you had a second degree connection to any bloggers through one of your first degree connections. If you did have a connection to that design industry blogger, you could ask for an introduction and you would have the opportunity to pitch your campaign and maybe get a mention or a feature story.

Another option in the relationship filter tool is to specify LinkedIn group members that fit your search criteria. This is extremely powerful because a member interested in the same industry as your crowdfunding campaign or who is in the same LinkedIn group may be more willing to help out than a random individual. LinkedIn is all about helping you generate warm leads, and lists of individuals who share some kind of common connection or interest with you.

2. Profile View and Analysis

When researching professionals, bloggers, or journalists that you intend to ask to support your campaign, be sure to pay special attention to their previous work experiences and skills.

When I was the head of business development for my previous company (in the recruitment software industry) I remember an instance when I was looking through the profile of someone I had just met at a charity networking event. We only had the chance to talk very briefly, but we seemed to develop great rapport.

The conversation was largely informal and after a long day at work, I didn't think to mention what I did or the kind of software my company provided. From his card, I saw that he was involved in the film industry. I didn't think anything of it until I got back to my computer and had a chance to look through his LinkedIn profile. Sure enough, he had past experience as a recruiter, had made a career change, and was now pursuing his passion in film. A few phone calls and meetings later, and we ended up landing a client because he introduced us to one of his previous employers. Lessons learned: Always check out past experience and interests. Also, don't be afraid to reach out!

3. Introductions, InMails and Interest Groups

Of all the correspondence you make, only a small percentage will reach and resonate with the intended audience, and a smaller percentage will lead to your call-to-action. This action could include: backing your campaign, writing about it, tweeting about it, or sharing it with their friends.

Asking for introductions, posting in LinkedIn groups, commenting on discussions, sending InMails, and sending messages to your existing network comprise the highest level of communication you can make. Not all introductions will work out and not all InMails will be answered. More importantly, if a large volume of quality action takes place, it will yield desired conversions or results.

4. Updates and Expanding Your Network

In the same way that Facebook or Twitter helps you reach an audience of followers and friends, LinkedIn updates can help you market your crowdfunding campaign to your professional connections. By promoting specific reward tiers, you can let your network know about the different ways they can support your campaign from "liking" or sharing, to pledging at lower, middle, or upper tiers.

I'd recommend that you constantly work to expand your professional network. It doesn't matter whether you are inviting people to connect with you on LinkedIn through email, looking on LinkedIn for people you may know, or exchanging business cards that have a link to your campaign or website—as long as your expanding your professional network, you're doing good work.

How to Drive More Traffic to Your Crowdfunding Campaign Using Pinterest

ANDREEA AYERS

Pinterest is a great social media tool that you can use to increase the awareness of your crowdfunding campaign.

Besides being one of the fastest growing social media networks ever, Pinterest also has something that most other social media networks don't have—users who are ready to spend money. According to Fast Company (pattylennon.com/power-of-pinterst) Pinterest users spend twice as much money (on products they find through Pinterest) as Facebook users. What this means is that Pinterest users are browsing Pinterest with an interest in discovering **and** buying something new.

What this means for your crowdfunding campaign is that Pinterest is a great network for you if you want to connect with people who are ready to spend money. Here are a few tips and strategies that you can implement right away to increase awareness of your crowdfunding campaign through Pinterest.

1. Create pin-worthy images.

Pinterest is all about visually appealing images, so when you create your graphics for your crowdfunding campaign, make sure that they are colorful and visually pleasing. Many studies show that graphics that have both text **and** an image are more likely to go viral on Pinterest. That means that each graphic you create should have text and a call to action (such as "Click here to support us" or "Click to donate").

Encourage your supporters to pin images from your campaign page, in addition to sharing the images on Facebook and Twitter. And if you already have a website, take a screenshot of your campaign page, post it on your website and ask your current visitors to share that image on Pinterest as well.

2. Pin your crowdfunding videos.

Did you know that in addition to pinning images, you can also pin videos on Pinterest? Pin your own crowdfunding videos and ask others to pin them as well. Another idea is to create video updates throughout your campaign and post those to Pinterest on a regular basis.

3. Create a "pin it to win it" contest.

Why not create a "pin it to win it" contest where you give away some of your campaign prizes to those who pin them on Pinterest? This is a great way to discover new backers because these contests often go viral on Pinterest. Make sure to have images for each one of your prizes and include the prize value on the image to cultivate more engagement.

Keep these tips in mind when promoting your next crowdfunding campaign and you'll start to get new backers and followers by leveraging the power of the fastest growing social media network in history.

Insta-Results with Instagram

SUE B. ZIMMERMAN

Instagram, like Pinterest, is one of the fastest growing social media platforms with over 150 million active monthly users! It's proven that people engage more through visuals and short messages than other formats, so using Instagram is a perfect way to attract followers and awareness to a crowd-funding campaign.

According to Kickstarter, "Kickstarter is full of projects, big and small, that are brought to life through the direct support of people like you." When the overarching goal is to bring a project to life, the best way to support that effort and drive traffic to the campaign is through images and video. There are a few simple ways you can attract your ideal following on Instagram to help raise funds for your project.

Humanize your project. Make your project real by introducing the people behind your vision. Show pictures of your team, behind-the-scenes photos, images from your team on-the-streets, or customers who are willing to share testimonials. People are more likely to support your project when they can relate to the people creating it. Use the Instagram video feature to quickly share company and project highlights or milestones with your followers. Create a buzz and have fun!

Use third party apps. There are some really great apps that can help your images stand out on Instagram. Standout images will cause people to pay attention. Thus, you can cultivate more awareness, buzz, and ultimately, more support! Use a text overlay application, for example, so you can write a call-to-action or identify team members directly on your images. The app Diptic will allow you to create a unique and completely customizable collage. Flipagram lets you create a fast-moving slideshow comprised of multiple images, which immediately grabs your follower's attention.

Run a contest. Social media junkies love contests. What better way to generate excitement than through a little friendly competition? When you make your project fun and competitive, you're sure to attract a loyal following. You can use hashtags to follow engagement and buzz and then share across multiple social media platforms, like Facebook, Twitter, or Pinterest to keep the momentum going!

Create a theme. Be sure to create a theme for your crowdfunding campaign on Instagram so all visuals are connected to the project. Similar to creating a brand for a business, all imagery you use for your campaign on Instagram should be consistent in look and feel. This will drive your message deeper and help your project stay top of mind in the hearts (and pockets) of your followers and fans. Use the online design platform Canva.com to help you create those branded images.

Use hashtags. Hashtags are the magic of Instagram and many other social networks. Create a hashtag identifier that's unique to your campaign and follow the conversation. You can also use hashtags to find followers who might be interested in your project. For instance, if your crowdfunding campaign is producing karate movie, search for other Instagram users who are talking about #karate #martialarts or #karatekid. Start following these people and they'll most likely start following you. This is the **best** way to attract new followers and help build awareness you might not have otherwise gained. In other words, find the conversation and join it!

Put a link in your bio. To ensure you're driving traffic to your crowdfunding project, include the link to your campaign in your Instagram bio. That's the only place on Instagram a URL is hyperlinked. Be sure to mention in your comments, "Click link in bio" to help drive viewers to your funding page. If you create any images, be sure to watermark them with the URL as well so if someone shares this image, a new supporter can find the campaign easily.

Ultimately, using images and video on Instagram to drive traffic to your crowdfunding campaign could be a ton of fun if you do it right. Most importantly, it can help you meet your fundraising goals.

It's possible that now that you've read these overviews you are a bit overwhelmed by social media. If you have the budget, consider hiring a social media expert or team to build your following before, during, and after your campaign.

You can find a list of recommended services at
pattylennon.com/services

Before your campaign, it's helpful to write the bulk of the social media posts you plan to use while the campaign is live. That way you have them ready-to-go; plus you will be able to use a scheduling system such as Hootsuite (pattylennon.com/hootsuite) to have social media going out even when you are sleeping!

Updates

While social media will continue to drive the flow of new visitors to your campaign, updates will keep your previous contributors engaged and ideally sharing your campaign with their inner circles.

Updates go out through your crowdfunding platform and only to those whom have either contributed to your campaign or left a comment. This is great news, because you have a curated list of people already invested in what you're doing. Keep them in the loop with anything new that's happening with your product, service, or project: e.g. press mentions, milestones, or new media.

Here are some ideas for updates:

- A short, fun, or caring video of you saying "thank you" to your contributors.

- Pictures related to your product, service, or project.

- Milestone thank you messages. For example, "Wow! We've just hit 30% of our goal and it's only day two—

you are amazing! Thank you so much for helping us reach towards our goal!"

- Calls for help. For example, "We have only one week to go and we still need to raise $2000. If each of our existing donors contributes $15, we will meet our goal. Can you think about donating a bit more or sharing our campaign with your friends and family?"

Update your campaign at least once per week while the campaign is live, and more if you have exciting news to share!

After your campaign is over, continue to keep your contributors up to date with your product, service, or project. Let them know how you are doing with reward distribution, and tell contributors and followers anything else they might be interested in. Remember, crowdfunding is a marketing vehicle, so keep the marketing mojo going long after you've reached your funding goal.

Your Communication Plan

We covered communication to your Inner Circle in Chapter Five. Additionally, plan to communicate with all the people you've met along the way that mentioned they'd like to stay updated on your campaign. If you're using an email management system like Constant Contact, you can pre-schedule these communications.

Three to Six Months Prior to Launch

You can begin mailing your list months in advance of the campaign. This is different than the way you communicate with your friends and family (aka your inner circle), as you should contact them one week before you launch your campaign. List communications will usually focus more on what you are crowdfunding rather than your crowdfunding campaign. For instance if you are crowdfunding your book, you might keep people up to date on the progress of book development or share snippets of what you are writing.

If you already have a list you email regularly, you can start dropping hints that you'll be doing something exciting in a few months that will give them a "unique opportunity" to be involved in the creation of your project.

Two Weeks to Three Months Prior to Launch

As you communicate with your list, start to be specific about your intentions to crowdfund your product, service, or project. This is a great time to conduct surveys to gain information on what rewards might be of interest to your list. You can also ask for help naming your project on your crowdfunding platform.

Definitely let your followers know when you expect to launch and the fact that you'd love their support. Be as vulnerable as possible in your communication. Express that you are excited, scared, and nervous in words that feel comfortable to you.

One Week Before Launch

Send an email letting your list know that the time of launch is almost here. Unlike the letter you send to your inner circle a week prior to launch, you'll want to keep this brief. You won't have to provide background on how you came to launch a crowdfunding campaign, because the recipients will already be up to speed on where you are in this process.

One Day Before Campaign

Send a brief email alerting your list that they will receive an email tomorrow with details on how to support your campaign.

Morning of your campaign

Email your list letting them know it's go time! On all of these emails, like any other communication you send to prospective contributors and supporters, be sure to *offer a clear call to action!*

Day One Contributors

As I mentioned in Chapter 5 it is important to have a list of people who are willing to commit a certain dollar amount toward funding on day one. For a campaign raising less than $15,000, plan to have $1000 in pledged donations. If you're looking at funding more than $15,000, add $1000 for each $10,000 extra in funding you're seeking.

You'll want to get on the phone with these contributors on day one, or at a minimum send them a personalized email and follow up by phone to confirm they are funding you.

Getting a solid donation amount on day one sends a strong signal to other contributors that this is a viable campaign.

Throughout the Campaign

Email your list a few more times throughout your campaign. If you are approaching a milestone you need their help with, state that and then restate how they can help.

If something exciting happens with your product, service, or project, email them with that information. Simply remind them that your campaign is active and invite them to contribute via the link to your campaign.

Always be sure to let them know when an exciting bonus reward becomes available to create some excitement around contributing!

Note: Whenever you provide your link use your custom domain name (as discussed in Chapter Two).

Blogs

Remember all that work you did during your likeability campaign? You read and commented on blogs that either you wrote, your target contributors wrote or were relevant to your target contributors.

Beginning four weeks prior to launch, reach out to the owners of those blogs to see if they will feature a guest blog post from you.

There are many ways to approach bloggers but a straightforward approach email with the following structure is a great choice:

- Tell the blogger you are a fan of their blog. Mention something specific about what they wrote so they know you are serious.

- Connect what your crowdfunding campaign is about to the content on their blog.

- Make the request. Ask them if they would feature a guest blog from you.

- Thank them for their consideration.

Follow up weekly if you don't hear from them. Popular blogs get tons of email traffic. Unless the owner has responded "No, thank you," you can assume they haven't seen your email or it got lost in the shuffle.

Forward the original email with language such as this:

"Last week I sent you the below email. I'm sure you get an overwhelming number of emails each day. I'd love the opportunity to write a guest blog post for your blog. Thank you for your consideration!"

If you want to add a bit more personality, go for it!

Once the blogger accepts your offer for a guest blog post, provide them the post as soon as possible. The post should tell a story, not ask people to visit your crowdfunding site. Most bloggers allow you to post a small bio below your blog. This is where you should link to your campaign using your custom domain name.

Also, provide any media you have that can enhance the post.

Finally, ask them when they expect to post it. Let them know you want to ensure you have social media ready to go so you can promote their blog feature. This lets them know you plan to send traffic to their site, which is always helpful to them.

Some bloggers have editorial calendars which are scheduled months in advance. It's possible that they may not be able to feature you during your campaign. As long as the communication between you and the blogger is friendly, feel free to ask them if there is any way they can squeeze you in while your campaign is live.

This is one of the places where it is important to have that custom domain, because that blog will be up long after your campaign is over. If you have a custom domain that has been redirected back to your product or project site, you will continue to get traffic from this blog post long after your campaign is over!

Your Website

You can use your own site to promote your campaign in the following three ways:

1. Write blog posts that tie into your campaign and point readers back to the campaign. It is important to be telling stories rather than "selling" your campaign. Here are some great blog ideas:

    • Discuss your journey through crowdfunding.

    • Talk about funny things that happen along the way ("We went live and my computer died. I had no idea what was happening—then I realized I was leaning on the power button!")

    • Explain your reasons for turning to the crowd for help.

    • Describe what it feels like to be out there asking for money.

2. Put a banner at the top of your website with a countdown to the end of your campaign.

3. Add a campaign widget to the sidebar of your site.

I am always impressed with the new and better ways people find to use their website to drive traffic to their crowdfunding campaign.

Remember, the best information on how to market your project lies within you. The purpose of this work is to give you some structure. Pass over anything that feels like it doesn't fit. Also, if you find a new and fun way to market your campaign, go for it!

CHAPTER EIGHT:
THE EASY MONEY MINDSET

Easy money starts with easy. Even if you are weeks or months away from your campaign, you've already done a significant amount of work to make it successful by following the chapters we've already covered. Reward yourself with a day off.

This isn't simply a suggestion on my part—consider this part of your homework! Getting into an all work and no play cycle makes for a grumpy crowdfunder; and no one likes a grumpy crowdfunder. Adding joy and pleasure to your life activates the energy of *easy money*.

Prosperity is your birthright, and abundance your soul's natural state of being. But, your soul's essence can get buried under all that hard work.

It's time to relax and play! For an entire day, feed your soul with relaxation and play.

It doesn't need to be perfect! Here are some options to consider for your day off:

- Eat good food.

- Spend time outdoors.

- Watch a funny movie.

- Read a book just for entertainment.

- Spend time with a good friend.

- Make something with your hands.

- Take a nap.

- Eat a delicious dessert **without** looking at
  the calories.

Even if you just wander through your day without an agenda, you will have done your homework. The point is to add some ease to your life.

Your Day Off

Ideally, you have days off every week, but I find that doesn't happen for most of us. Even if we aren't technically *working* on our work, we are working in some other way—with our children, home, parents, or on special projects. Schedule a day away from all of this—to just be.

Scheduling isn't very romantic, but it is necessary. Write down when your day off will take place here:

My day off will take place on: _____

Now go block it off in your calendar. If you think you may end up spending the day stressed out, trying to come up with something peaceful and relaxing to do, be sure to write a list of things you might want to do ahead of time—that way you don't have to do any thinking.

Things I might like to do on my day off:_____

_____

_____

_____

Once you have had your day off you can return to your work refreshed and renewed!

It is normal to resist taking a day off before you've actually launched your campaign. the more intense the resistance to taking a day off, the more benefit you will get from it. If you resist taking the day off, just understand that resistance is a pretty good indicator of how much good will come of your day off if you give yourself the chance.

We live in a world that moves at a frenetic pace. Multi-tasking has become a way of life. We are always go-go-going. Our bodies and minds were not designed for this pace. Your wellbeing requires rest. Your *soul* requires rest. Oh yeah, I said it—the "s" word—soul.

If you were attracted to the marketing benefits of this book you are likely doing work that is tied to your life's work. It's your purpose. It's your mission. And when we start throwing around words like "purpose" and "mission" we are talking at a soul level.

The reason I'm so passionate about crowdfunding is that for the first time human beings that are doing good work in the world can talk openly and honestly about it **and** receive money in support of it!

You have important work to do here on this planet. I want your campaign to succeed. I want **you** to succeed! When more of the good guys and good gals start succeeding, our world becomes a better place. That success is more likely if you launch your campaign well rested and refreshed!

The Dynamics of "Easy"

When you are doing the work you came to do on this planet, money flows to you easily—if you allow it to. If you believe it has to be hard, it will be hard. If you allow it to be easy it will be easy. The way to make that happen is to experience *easy* now. That experience includes giving yourself some time off.

The universe has your back. It will support you. It will also follow your lead. You show it what you want through your thoughts, words, and actions. It delivers to you exactly what you are thinking, speaking, and acting out.

When you *work, work, work* and never take a break, the universe delivers more of that stress and overwhelm to your doorstep. When you give yourself room to breathe and honor your need to rest, the universe will deliver more ease to your doorstep.

I'm not asking you to take my word for it. Try it out yourself. Give yourself the space of a day to just be. Relax. Do something enjoyable. Do lots of things that are enjoyable. Then watch. You will see the magic.

Speaking of magic, what would you say if I told you I could make hidden contributors magically appear?

Uncovering Hidden Contributors

You have hidden contributors. Your hidden contributors aren't hiding from *you*—you are hiding from *them*. They are the people or groups of people you are afraid to reach out to.

Hiding from these potential contributors is one of the ways you make this process hard on yourself. We all do it. We don't want to look foolish or be too presumptive about who will help us.

Remember in Chapter Four when we talked about how money surfaces people's concerns? Hiding from potential contributors is an example of how this plays out in many crowdfunders' campaigns. I have yet to meet one crowdfunder who didn't have at least one person they considered asking but then thought twice about it.

We worry what people will think. We fear their rejection. And so we don't ask at all. In some cases you might completely block out whole groups of funders.

We make it hard when it could be easy. I say "we" because I was right there with you and every other person who has the courage to launch a crowdfunding campaign. When you launch a crowdfunding campaign you are putting yourself out there is a **BIG** way. And **BIG** can be scary for us.

Human beings fear social rejection. This seems illogical in today's day and age. However, from an evolutionary perspective it makes total sense to a part of our brain that evolved from the early days of humankind. In caveman days we needed our tribe to keep us safe. We hunted in packs. We found safety in numbers. Rejection meant sure death. So when the amygdala—the region in your brain responsible for the fight-or-flight response—registers that you are putting yourself in a position to be socially rejected it screams "RETREAT! RETREAT!"

You can condition your brain to understand that when you request help it's a good thing but I'd need a whole book to cover that topic. For now, I just want you to understand when you feel the need to avoid requesting help from potential contributors, it is based on a fear response that dates back to caveman days and not your current reality.

I'll tell you there is one tried and true way to condition your fear-focused amygdala to understand that asking for help is not something you need to flee from. That is: to experience positive emotions as a result of asking for help. When support and contributions start flowing into your crowdfunding campaign you will experience some great positive emotions—like excitement, elation, love, peace, or joy.

And there is more good news. The universe responds to **big** actions in kind. Asking for help requires courage. If you show courage, your courage is rewarded. You are rewarded with money. You are rewarded with confidence (because let me tell you that you will feel like a rock star when you succeed at crowdfunding!) And, you are rewarded with the knowledge that what you are doing in the world is wanted, needed, and supported by others. That knowledge will fuel you in powerful ways as you walk this sometimes lonely journey of creation. Whether you are an entrepreneur, writer, or inventor this knowledge can help you feel good about your project.

Here's the deal. When you ask people for help, they either will help or they won't. They are not rejecting **you**. They may not want what you are offering, but so what? You haven't created your project or product to serve everyone. You've created your project or product to serve a particular group of people. If someone doesn't contribute, it is about that person and not about you. That person may be experiencing money issues. He or she could be overwhelmed. That's no reflection on you and you have every right to ask!

Now it's possible that even after this pep talk your amygdala may still be hiding a few contributors from you in the hopes that you just don't put yourself out there to that person or group. If that is the case then I offer you one final line of defense. I have created a meditation that I use in my Crowdfund with Ease™ program to bypass that silly little amygdala and get to the creative powerhouse part of your brain.

As my gift to you for purchasing this book
you can access it here:
pattylennon.com/money-meditation
Use code: EASYMONEY

The reason I'm sharing this here is because if you have gotten this far in the book I know you are committed to this journey and I want to honor that commitment with a gift.

In the Crowdfund with Ease™ Program people have been blown away by what they uncovered with this meditation. It is my personal mission to help you—and everyone else out there who is living their purpose—recognize and access the universal support available to you as you walk your path. I believe this meditation is one way to do this.

If you haven't done a lot of work with guided meditation you will be amazed to learn how much information is available to you when you aren't spending all your time in your logical, thinking brain. If you *have* worked with guided meditations before then you probably understand the power they hold, so I'll simply say—enjoy!

Once you have completed the meditation use the space below to capture what you find.

1. _____

2. _____

3. _____

4. _____

It's possible that you uncover a funder that didn't feel hidden—you already had them on your radar and were intending to reach out. If that's the case, a part of you is telling you that you may have had some resistance to reaching out to them. That's ok—you know it now and can move forward.

It's also possible that symbols or representations of your hidden contributors show up in the meditation. You may not recognize these symbols or representations at first. Try not to analyze what you see. Write it down and also jot down the first person or group that pops into your head if you see something like this. If you are blank, just give it some time. It will "pop," and when it does you can return to complete the exercise.

Now, write down three ways you'll reach out to each hidden contributor before, during, or (in some cases) after your campaign to generate funding and support for your business, project, or event. You can use the following template to explain how you'll reach out to these contributors.

Hidden Contributor #1

1. _____

2. _____

3. _____

Hidden Contributor #2

1. _____

2. _____

3. _____

Hidden Contributor #3

1. _____

2. _____

3. _____

Hidden Contributor #4

1. _____

2. _____

3. _____

Hidden Contributor #5

1. _____

2. _____

3. _____

This is one place in the Crowdfund with Ease™ program where participants find benefit in the support of a buddy or group. If you are feeling anxious about reaching out to these contributors or any of your other potential contributors find someone to support you through this process. Tell them about the groups or individuals that really excite you, and the people you want to pursue but feel scared or resistant to do so.

Let that person support you and encourage you!

CHAPTER NINE
GET READY,
GET SET...LAUNCH!

In the previous chapters I introduced you to all the building blocks you need to create a successful crowdfunding campaign. You may be overwhelmed. This is normal. If someone had simply told me from day one how much work would be required of me I probably never would have taken the first step. But that would have been a huge mistake.

And here is why—crowdfunding will transform you and your business in ways you cannot fathom right now. Our tech-dependent world can get pretty lonely, especially if you are an entrepreneur, writer, or inventor. You are always in charge and it's easy to feel like the weight of the world is on your shoulders.

If you are like I was: some days you wake up and just wish you had a bit more support. You'd like to know that someone has your back. And if you are living your purpose through your work, you'd probably like to know that someone besides you cares about what you are doing and believes in you.

That is how I felt before crowdfunding. That all changed when I launched my crowdfunding campaign.

Imagine waking up one morning and realizing you have an entire team of people cheering you on. You get out of bed, head downstairs for your morning coffee, and open your computer to twenty emails from people telling you how amazing you are.

In fact, you are so amazing that they want to support you in what you are doing. Money flows into your bank account every hour from these same people. They are so excited about what you are doing they tell all their friends. And then their friends tell their friends, and so on. Soon people who never even knew you existed now know who you are.

And even better, not only do they know you, but they also understand your mission on a deep level. You are seen like never before, and because people now understand what you are doing and, more importantly, *why* you are doing it, your support grows and grows.

Doors that were shut suddenly open. Conversations about your product or business that were stalled, now resume. TV, magazines, and blogs you have pitched for months or years suddenly want to feature you.

You have a story. Crowdfunding allows you to tell that story in a way people can hear it, understand it, and share it. And that makes the work we discussed in these chapters go from feeling like "A LOT OF WORK" to feeling like you have just been given a gift you are excited to unwrap!

On the days leading up to the launch of my crowdfunding campaign I was scared, nervous and excited all at once. I paced. I worked. I made last minute calls to secure day one support. People had said they would support me, but there was a tiny, scared part of me that wondered whether they would really show up the way they had promised.

The morning my campaign started I got up early so I could get the kids ready for school and be prepared when my campaign went live. I was sitting at our dining room table staring at the computer as my campaign launched. "Would anyone show up?" I wondered. It felt as if the world stopped and there I was suspended in time. I wasn't sure I would be able to breathe again until the first contribution came in.

Just then my kids came running down the stairs. "It's time! It's time! Your thing is going! We want to be the first!" They raced over to me, and handed me crumpled dollar bills from their piggy banks.

They dropped the bills on my computer and said proudly "We are your first funders!" It is hard to put into words what that moment meant to me. After that, everything changed. A huge fear was lifted from me. I remembered that I already had so much.

I remembered how many people I already had in my life that supported me (when I just gave them a chance).

And you will have that moment too. Someone will show up in such a big way for you that you will realize you are loved, you are supported, and you are not alone.

Over the course of my campaign, word spread about what I was doing. Organizations contacted me that wanted to be aligned with the Mom Gets A Business Conference—the conference I was funding with that campaign. Many of those conversations turned into sponsorships. I was featured in newspapers and online. Every moment of every day something new was happening around the conference and it was all because of my crowdfunding campaign.

It all moved at the speed of light and it was a blast. On day fourteen we hit our funding goal and at that point all the funds that were sitting on hold at Indiegogo were released into my account. I watched PayPal as the contributions poured in.

Now that was fun!

It wasn't until it was all over and I could catch my breath that I was able to look back and take in all that had transpired over the course of the thirty days that I ran my campaign.

I started out thinking I was launching a campaign to raise the $45,000 to launch a conference that my heart told me many, many women needed. What I got was so much more.

I discovered that crowdfunding is the most powerful marketing machine available to us today. The reach and awareness I gained with this campaign could not have happened any other way. I realized the breathtaking amount of love and support that surrounded me. The money is just a symptom of something so much bigger that happens when you launch a campaign.

Successful crowdfunding requires that you stand strongly, state clearly what you are doing and why you are doing it and then ask for support. That is a powerful combination that creates powerful results! This hasn't just been my experience. This continues to be the experience my clients tell me they have as well.

However, not every person that launches a crowdfunding campaign has this experience. Many people fail. There is one requirement to succeed: You must go all-in.

Going all-in means doing the work to get your message clear and convey it in a way that people can understand. Going all-in means you put yourself out there and you ask for help.

I talk to people every week who have crowdfunding campaigns that have failed. They are discouraged with the process and are unclear about what they did wrong. I know what happened—they didn't go all-in. It's not their fault. In many cases they didn't understand what it took to go all-in. In other cases they were scared and didn't get their message out there in the biggest way possible. Some others just didn't ask for the support they needed.

You are not going to be one of them and here is why. You have this book and they didn't. (See that! You are already on your way to success just by having this little book in your hands!)

Because you've read this book you know what it takes to be all-in. You see what is required and by now realize it probably makes sense to get help with some parts of your campaign. That way you won't be alone.

So what's next for you?

If you are ready to harness the power of crowdfunding, the next step is a pretty easy one. It's time to figure out what you are going to do on your own, what you need help with, and how are you going to get that help.

All this stuff is stuff you can do on your own. But that can be pretty exhausting if you have priorities outside launching your campaign.

When I laid out the plan for my campaign I looked for ways that I could outsource pieces of the process to make it fit into the schedule my life and family demanded. I didn't do all of it on my own . I made a strategic investment in resources that made sense for me. You will do the same. You probably will not invest in the same ways I did. Your story will look different based on your skill set and resources.

For instance, if you have more time than money you may want to do it all yourself with the support of some friends and family. If you have a tight deadline you will likely want to outsource more of the process.

If you want to do it yourself and you'd enjoy access to templates that guide you gently through the process, along with a supportive community of people also preparing to launch their campaigns then my Crowdfund with Ease™ program is a helpful option.

Perhaps you like a lot of handholding. At the time I launched my campaign I didn't know of anyone who was guiding people through the process of launching a crowdfunding campaign. But now I do. If you'd like this type of individualized attention, you can check out a list of certified consultants here:

For more information on these services visit
pattylennon.com/services

Maybe you want a middle ground between doing it all yourself and having someone guide you every step of the way. That is an option, as well.

There are many components to launching a campaign. The right solution for you may be getting help with some components and doing some on your own. Let's walk through the areas where you may benefit from support so you can decide what you want to do on your own and where you'd like to get support.

Research: At different points in your campaign there will be a need to do research. For example, looking at the various platforms, finding campaigns that spark your interest, and finding out where your funders spend their time. Because research can be personal, it's best if you do most of this; still, a trained assistant can help cut down the amount of time you invest in research.

Video Creation: This is the heart and soul of your campaign. Your budget will dictate what support you can get in this process. Investing in this process can look like hiring a full production team, working with a video producer to guide you through your own process, and hiring a videographer to film you with a high quality camera. Or it can simply mean investing in good equipment so you have high quality lighting and sound.

Social Media: Social media plays a critical role in the success of your campaign. Becoming active on social media, engaging in your likeability campaign, writing social media for the various stages of your campaign, and scheduling social posts are all activities that can be handled by a social media consultant or highly trained virtual assistant.

Written Communications: As we've discussed, communicating regularly with your contributors, potential contributors, and supporters is important. Written communication includes emails, campaign updates, and prewritten copy. Although you will want to personalize your communications, a skilled copywriter will be able to create most of these communications. If written communications is a challenge for you, a copywriter may be a sound investment.

Marketing: Throughout this book, I've explained each piece of your marketing plan—from creating your list of target contributor groups, to your pitch video and communication plan. I can show you what to do and how to do it, but I can't do it for you. (If I could I would!) In my private business coaching practice I love working with entrepreneurs and creative types to develop marketing plans and materials that work for them.

Every person is different. You may not feel comfortable with marketing your campaign exactly as it's laid out in this book. That is ok. Be true to who you are. If you feel like getting support in developing marketing materials, there are a number of business coaches that can help you with this process. Just be sure they understand how crowdfunding works so you both move in the same direction!

Reward Design: Designing your rewards is an extension of your marketing process. In Chapter Six I shared my 3D process for reward creation. These rewards are key to converting many visitors to your campaign into contributors. A good reward will draw attention to your campaign and excite people. This is something I found challenging to do on my own but, as I mentioned in Chapter Six, if you grab a few supportive friends and serve some great drinks, brainstorming has all the makings of a party! This is one place in the process that I urge you to get help. Bouncing ideas off other people will help you generate the juiciest rewards possible.

Administration: Throughout the campaign you'll want to regularly check the campaign site for new contributions and comments so that you can respond in a timely manner to supporters. You will also want to watch social media sites for people who are sharing your campaign so you can repost their shares and thank them. Additionally there is content to be loaded to the campaign site before you launch and each time you do an update. This can be very time consuming. You may want to solicit the help of a friend or assistant to be an extra set of "eyes" in this process so you are not glued to your computer.

Media Outreach: Reaching out to bloggers, local and national newspapers, and television networks can elevate the visibility of your campaign. There are PR consultants that do this for a living. In our Crowdfund with Ease™ program we dive a bit deeper into how to pitch the press on your own so media outreach is definitely something *you* can do. If you are looking to generate a significant amount of contributions from strangers this may be a good place to invest in a PR consultant who has experience creating visibility for people and products in a short amount of time through media.

Project Planning: As you start this process, lay out each task in your project so that you have a plan to take you from start to finish. Assign dates to each task so you are clear on deliverables. This is especially important when you are including team members that may need to conclude a task before another can begin. Project planning is a skill anyone can have but not everyone wants to have. If you have a hyper-organized friend that loves creating lists and schedules this may be the perfect support person for this task.

I use Basecamp (**basecamp.com**) to do all my project planning.

Beyond Basecamp, there are plenty of cloud-based systems that make planning easy. In the Crowdfund with Ease™ Program I give participants a template that lays out each task so Project Planning is a simple data entry process.

To get you started in determining which parts you will do on your own and where you will get support I created this really simple checklist. If you complete no other worksheets in this book, at least fill out the checklist below:

	Do it on my own (y/n)	Need Support (y/n)	Places I can get support
Research			
Video Creation			
Written Communications			
Marketing			
Reward Design			
Administration			
Media Outreach			
Project Planning			

A printable version of this worksheet is available at **pattylennon.com/worksheets**

I know this all feels big—but that is because this is big stuff! You have an incredible gift to share with the world, a solution that will help improve people's lives and that solution, that gift, needs money to grow. You deserve to access the money to make that gift grow!

More importantly your people want to know about what you are doing. Crowdfunding is your key to getting the word out about what you are doing and allowing the people in your community and beyond to support you in doing that.

Reach down deep inside your mind right now. Find that spark that brought your idea to life. Feel how powerful it is. It is time for you to bring what is inside of you into the world in a grander way. The world needs it! The world needs YOU!

Each of us holds a piece of the puzzle to make this world better. The only way we can make the world better is if we each honor our gifts—if we make our piece of the puzzle known. Crowdfunding will help you do that.

I got the funding I needed for my Mom Grows A Business Conference and received so much more in the process of crowdfunding. Now it's time to bring *your* dream to life. I know you can do this. Let's show the world what you've got!

RESOURCES

Introduction

Information on Ubuntu Edge:

pattylennon.com/ubuntu

Chapter 1

Searching for crowdfunding platforms: CrowdsUnite.com

CrowdsUnite is the largest user review website in the world for crowdfunding platforms. Their goal is to gather the essential information about the platforms in one location. There are filter options that allow you to search for the platforms that you qualify for then sort and compare these platforms side-by-side.

Business planning program:
pattylennon.com/plan

Purchase business cards:
- vistaprint.com
- uprinting.com
- zazzle.com

Reserve Custom Domain Names:

- godaddy.com
- 1and1.com
- domainname.com

Find email management systems at:

pattylennon.com/constant-contact

Chapter 3

Articles on DIY scripting:

pattylennon.com/write-video-script

pattylennon.com/storyboard-tips

Video production:

pattylennon.com/sharethesizzle

Finding stock video:

pattylennon.com/stock-video

Chapter 8

You can find social media consultants, copywriters, and crowdfunding consultants at: pattylennon.com/services

Chapter 9

An example of cloud-based project planning:

basecamp.com

Crowdfund with Ease™ Program:

pattylennon.com/CFWE

CONTRIBUTORS

Alex Feldman CrowdsUnite.com

Alex Feldman helps small businesses raise money online. He is the CEO of CrowdsUnite, which is the number one review site for building funding for websites. Publications including the Huffington Post have mentioned Alex and his achievements. Major websites like crowdsourcing.org published his writings on crowdfunding. Also, Vator.TV interviewed him about helping small businesses with funding. Alex also runs monthly crowdfunding networking events in New York City, a program with over 400 members.

Crystal Girgenti

Crystal Girgenti is a technology and online business consultant who has helped many small business owners launch and grow their businesses with the use of online marketing and technology.

Salvador Briggman

CrowdCrux.com

Salvador Briggman is the founder of CrowdCrux.com, a blog that helps creators launch crowdfunding projects on websites like Kickstarter and Indiegogo. He is also the owner of KickstarterForum.org, and recently launched a new website, PitchFuse.com, which aims to help creators gather a following before they launch a crowdfunding project.

Blane Friest

http://www.ddmproduction.com

For over two decades, DDM Production has been creating multimedia events that thrill and educate. During this period, Blane Friest, Founder and Executive Producer of DDM Production, has spent time as a consultant at Morgan Stanley and produced hundreds of events, working closely with top CEOs and government officials, as well as luminaries like Martha Stewart and Hillary Clinton.

Andreea Ayers

LaunchGrowJoy.com

As the founder of LaunchGrowJoy.com Andreea loves to inspire and share! She loves to help other entrepreneurs succeed, whether it's through online courses, speaking at events across the country, leading webinars or writing guest articles. Andreea has created massive success through strategic marketing plans including Pinterest, Affiliate Marketing and Targeted PR.

Sue B. Zimmerman

SuebZimmerman.com

Sue B. Zimmerman, aka the #InstagramGal and #TheInstagramExpert, is an online business promotional expert and a master at Instagram. She is a speaker and business coach. She is the founder of SueB.Do & Sue B. Zimmerman Enterprise.

ACKNOWLEDGEMENTS

This book, like everything I have ever created or completed, exists because of the amazing people in my life. I am deeply grateful for the love and support I have.

At the top of that list are my children. Matthew and Katie, you were my very first funders. Your faith in me kept me going on the days I wanted to give up, and it continues to make every success so much sweeter. I love you both. Thank you.

My sweet husband, Matt, put up with me on my most stressed-out days and picked up the slack so that I could finish this book. Matt, for this and so many, many other reasons I know I am a lucky, lucky gal.

Angela Lauria, my publisher knew this book was inside of me before I did, and she made sure I brought it into the world. I owe special thanks to her amazing team that worked behind the scenes to bring this book to life. Journey Grrrl Publishing—thank you!

To my Savor Sisters: Angela Jia Kim, who has always pushed me to embrace goals that felt too big and go out there and make them happen; Michelle Lange, the very first person to whisper the word "crowdfunding" to me and my Savor Circle Sisters—Payson, Kat, Justine, Janice, Rosemary, Michelle, Jodi, Shasta and Jennifer—who cheered me on through my first crowdfunding campaign and then through my first crowdfunding book. You ladies rock!

And finally and most importantly a big fat THANK YOU to the Big U! Every part of this life is a gift including the opportunity to write. I endeavor to honor this privilege by living with a grateful heart.

ABOUT THE AUTHOR

Before launching two successful businesses, Patty Lennon, M.S. enjoyed a 15-year career at one of the world's largest banks, Citigroup. Promoted to VP at a young age she learned early on that an entrepreneurial attitude creates success in every environment.

In 2010 Patty founded Mom Gets A Life® in response to a need she saw in mothers of young children. Her multi-media company hosts sold out events to cheering crowds throughout the year including the Mom Gets a Business® Conference, which launched in 2012.

In 2013 Patty founded Crowdfund with Ease™, a training company dedicated to sharing the valuable business growth potential and marketing strategies Patty uncovered while running her own crowdfunding campaign in 2012.

Patty is a national speaker and author who inspires audiences to lead and sell with passion and purpose. She is an expert business coach and she teaches businesses and individuals to develop working business plans, balance dreams with action, and produce transformational events that create real sales.

Patty Lennon lives in Danbury, CT with her husband and two children. She loves adventures in any form and believes adding wine, chocolate and gratitude to anything makes it better. To find out where Patty's up to visit PattyLennon. com.

In two years we've created over 134 bestselling books in a row, 90% from first-time authors. We do this by selecting the highest quality and highest potential applicants for our future programs.

Our program doesn't just teach you how to write a book—our team of coaches, developmental editors, copy editors, art directors, and marketing experts incubate you from book idea to published bestseller, ensuring that the book you create can actually make a difference in the world. Then we give you the training you need to use your book to make the difference you want to make in the world, or to create a business out of serving your readers. If you have life-or world-changing ideas or services, a servant's heart, and the willingness to do what it REALLY takes to make a difference in the world with your book, go to http://theauthorincubator.com/apply/ to complete an application for the program today.

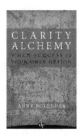

Clarity Alchemy: When Success Is Your Only Option

by Ann Bolender

Cracking the Code: A Practical Guide to Getting You Hired

by Molly Mapes

Divorce to Divine: Becoming the Fabulous Person You Were Intended to Be

by Cynthia Claire

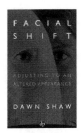

Facial Shift: Adjusting to an Altered Appearance

by Dawn Shaw

Finding Clarity: Design a Business You Love and Simplify Your Marketing

by Amanda H. Young

Flourish: Have It All Without Losing Yourself

by Dr. Rachel Talton

Marketing To Serve: The Entrepreneur's Guide to Marketing to Your Ideal Client and Making Money with Heart and Authenticity

by Cassie Parks

NEXT: How to Start a Successful Business That's Right for You and Your Family

by Caroline Greene

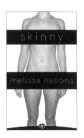

Pain Free: How I Released 43 Years of Chronic Pain

by Dottie DuParcé (Author), John F. Barnes (Foreword)

Secret Bad Girl: A Sexual Trauma Memoir and Resolution Guide

by Rachael Maddox

Skinny: The Teen Girl's Guide to Making Choices, Getting the Thin Body You Want, and Having the Confidence You've Always Dreamed Of

by Melissa Nations

The Aging Boomers: Answers to Critical Questions for You, Your Parents and Loved Ones

by Frank M. Samson

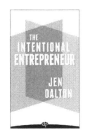

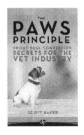

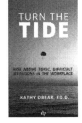

The Incubated Author: 10 Steps to Start a Movement with Your Message

by Angela Lauria

The Intentional Entrepreneur: How to Be a Noisebreaker, Not a Noisemaker

by Jen Dalton (Author), Jeanine Warisse Turner (Foreword)

The Paws Principle: Front Desk Conversion Secrets for the Vet Industry

by Scott Baker

Turn the Tide: Rise Above Toxic, Difficult Situations in the Workplace

by Kathy Obear

35995502R00121

Made in the USA
Middletown, DE
21 October 2016